RUNNING THE COAST FOR A CURE
ONE MAN'S JOURNEY FOR HIS NIECE WITH STURGE-WEBER SYNDROME

Thank you for your support!

Al DiCesari

RUNNING THE COAST FOR A CURE

ONE MAN'S JOURNEY FOR HIS NIECE WITH STURGE-WEBER SYNDROME

AL DECESARIS

Copyright © 2014 - 2019 by **Al DeCesaris**

All rights reserved. No part of this publication may be reproduced, distributed or transmitted in any form or by any means, without prior written permission.

Al DeCesaris
www.aldecesaris.com

Front Cover Image © 2014 by Shawn Vernon

Back Cover Image © 2016 by Bill Whitcher

Cover Design © 2016 by Little Bit Heart

Book Layout © 2016 BookDesignTemplates.com

Running The Coast For A Cure: One Man's Journey For His Niece With Sturge-Weber Syndrome / Al DeCesaris -- 1st ed.

ISBN-13: 978-0692687598

ISBN-10: 0692687599

To my sister Ida

Your love for Jenna and your determination to improve the quality of her life are an inspiration to all.

**All profits from the sale of this book fund
Sturge-Weber syndrome research**

To help further the efforts to find a cure, purchase
Al DeCesaris' first book, *Crossing America For A Cure:
A Bicycle Journey Of Inspiration And Hope*. The book
chronicles his 3,088-mile solo cross-country bike ride to
raise awareness and funds for Sturge-Weber research.

What is the use of living, if it be not to strive for noble
causes and to make this muddled world a better place
for those who will live in it after we are gone?

Winston Churchill

Foreword

When I first met Al DeCesaris, he was putting his mind and body through more than I could have ever imagined putting myself through while I was playing 13 years in the NFL. He, was nearing the home stretch of an unsupported coast-to-coast bicycle ride. Unsupported! That means he was out there by himself. He didn't have a support crew riding behind him in a van like you see on TV. If it was not on his bike, he didn't have it. Al was on the most incredible journey I could think of.

What I didn't understand was how big of an effect it would have on me and others in the Sturge-Weber community. My oldest daughter has Sturge-Weber syndrome. For so many families affected by this disease, his journey gave a reason for hope and a belief that things will be better tomorrow. Here was Al pushing the limits of mankind to spread awareness about this rare disease that has affected us so very deeply.

His efforts stoked my competitive fire that had all but been gone since I retired from the NFL. I had been doing some running and was thinking about signing up for a half-marathon. But after meeting him, I decided that I couldn't just do what was possible, I had to try what seemed impossible. Al inspires us to push each day exactly where I left off the day before, I would cover every mile (every foot actually) down the coast.

Now, it's no secret I've never been much of an athlete. And I didn't have the running experience that would lead one to believe I could accomplish something this ambitious. In fact, even though I planned to run close to a marathon a day, I'd never actually run a marathon. Still, I have something within me that I knew would make this seemingly impossible task achievable – purpose. My purpose is my desire to help my beautiful young niece Jenna live a better life. For her and because of her, I am inspired to fight Sturge-Weber syndrome on her behalf.

Jenna is the youngest child of my sister Ida and her husband Ed. She's playful, spunky, and perseverant, and has a smile that lights up her face. Yet, even with her high-spiritedness and determination, because of her medical condition Jenna has had a very difficult life.

Sturge-Weber syndrome is a congenital, neurological disorder that causes abnormal blood vessels to develop in the skin, eyes, and on the surface of the brain. Although it manifests differently in each person affected, for Jenna it has resulted in a pronounced port-wine birthmark on the right side of her face (from her hairline to the lower part of her cheek) and glaucoma in her right eye. Despite the severe problems these conditions present, it's the abnormal blood vessels on the surface of her brain that pose the greatest threat because they often lead to other serious health complications including seizures, strokes and stroke-like episodes, impaired motor coordination, paralysis, developmental delays, learning disabilities, mental retardation, migraines, mood and behavior problems, and even death.

Over the years, Jenna has suffered debilitating seizures and stroke-like episodes, which have left her physically and mentally impaired. To see her suffer on a daily basis is heartbreaking. Yet, her bravery and resilience, as well as Ida's tireless and unwavering dedication to her well-being, are truly inspiring.

With Ida leading the way, not long after Jenna was diagnosed, my family and I began our volunteer efforts to create awareness and raise funds for the research and treatment of Sturge-Weber syndrome. Since then, we have hosted numerous charity events which have created considerable awareness and raised over $1,000,000. This money has directly supported the work of the Hunter Nelson Sturge-Weber Center at Kennedy Krieger Institute, and helped fund research that led to the discovery of the cause of Sturge-Weber syndrome.

Since shortly after her birth, Jenna has been in the care of Anne Comi, M.D., the Director of the Hunter Nelson Sturge-Weber Center and co-author of the research that produced the ground-breaking discovery. According to Dr. Comi and the other senior authors: Jonathan Pevsner, Ph.D., Professor in the Department of Neurology at Kennedy Krieger Institute, and Douglas A. Marchuk, Ph.D., Director of Molecular Genetics and Microbiology at Duke University School of Medicine, Sturge-Weber syndrome and port-wine birthmarks are caused by a somatic activating mutation in the *GNAQ* gene. "This is a complete game changer for those with Sturge-Weber syndrome and the millions born with port-wine birthmarks," said Dr. Comi. "Now that we know the underlying genetic mutation responsible for both conditions, we're hopeful that we can move quickly towards targeted therapies, offering families the promise of new treatments for the first time." Although much more research must be done, the study, published on May 8, 2013 in the *New England Journal of Medicine*, brings researchers closer than ever to a cure. "This is a giant step forward," said Dr. Comi. "We have real hope in the next five to ten years, perhaps sooner, perhaps a little longer, that there will be...new treatments and perhaps even a cure for Sturge-Weber syndrome."

Notwithstanding the progress that has been made, because Sturge-Weber syndrome is so rare (affecting only 1 in 20,000 individuals) funding for research has been difficult to obtain. For this reason, raising private funds to support ongoing research is critical.

With the hope that this event would help the doctors continue their vital work, I set out to run the coast. Now, I didn't know what the journey would bring, 20 miles and a major injury or 2,000 miles and a successful run all the way to Key Largo, Florida. But I did know that as long as my body would allow, I'd continue to put in the miles each day for Jenna and all those suffering with Sturge-Weber syndrome so that a cure may one day be found.

Al DeCesaris

Day 1 (9/8/14): Lubec, ME to Whiting, ME [18.5 miles]

I can do this, I told myself as I strapped my hydration pack onto my back and made my way over to the red-and-white striped lighthouse that was my run's starting location. *I know I can.* This is the ambitious athletic endeavor I dreamt up. This is what I trained for, what I chose to do for my 10-year-old niece Jenna. I believe it's something that will bring her hope, something that will make a difference.

Well, there I was in Lubec, Maine, on foot and alone, about to begin my East Coast charity run in honor of Jenna and all those living with Sturge-Weber syndrome. A 2,000-some-odd mile solo run to raise awareness and funds for Sturge-Weber research, and to further the efforts to find a cure for this devastating disorder.

The locals say Lubec is where the sun first rises. Since it's the easternmost town in the contiguous United States, I'd say they have a fair claim to that assertion. And if the clear blue sky was any indication, today's sunrise was a spectacular one. I must admit, I wasn't there to see it myself. Even though this was the first day of what may be the most important endeavor of my life, I'm not a morning person and a ceremonial 5:59am sunrise was *not* happening. However, when I did arrive at my starting location, Lubec's Quoddy Head State Park, the sun was still low in the sky and danced on the coastal waters assuaging my nerves and filling me with optimism.

I chose the park, specifically the park's West Quoddy Head Lighthouse, as my starting location because it's the easternmost point in the northernmost state on the East Coast. It didn't hurt that the lighthouse overlooks the Quoddy Narrows and the Bay of Fundy and has scenic views of Sail Rock and the Canadian island of Grand Manan in the distance.

The way I looked at it, if my non-marathon running, inexperienced self is going to run some 2,000-miles through 14 states down the entire East Coast, I want to have at least a few quality photos of myself — looking happy and healthy — against an amazing backdrop. What better place and what better time than there at the start because once this outlandish adventure begins, and the miles take their toll on me, there's no telling what the scenery, or I will look like.

As I surveyed the lighthouse grounds wondering what the next few months had in store for me, I met a couple from Alabama. I don't recall exactly what I said to them (call it adrenaline, nerves, or just an aging brain), but I did tell them about Jenna and her challenges. By the end of the conversation, I do believe the cause had two new supporters, and Jenna had two new fans.

Soon after, I was joined by Maine Representative Katherine Cassidy, a group of local residents, and reporters J.D. Rule and Chessie Crowe Gartmayer from

The Quoddy Tides. I had spoken to Katherine prior to arriving in Maine and she promised a proper Lubec send-off. Well, she delivered – everyone there was kind and encouraging and made this momentous occasion even more memorable. Their support also helped get my mind off the enormity of the day.

Al DeCesaris at Quoddy Head State Park in Lubec, Maine
(photo courtesy of Chessie Crowe Gartmayer).

Al DeCesaris

I then stretched my legs and readied for the start. Of course, I made sure not to forget to pose for the scrapbook-worthy "happy and healthy" photos. Before setting out, I rested my hand on the granite marker next to the lighthouse, which reads "easternmost point in the U.S.A.," then began my *Running The Coast For A Cure* East Coast charity run.

The road that ran from the park toward Lubec proper afforded me fantastic views of Passamaquoddy Bay, an inlet of the Bay of Fundy, and the Canadian province of New Brunswick beyond it. The terrain was hilly though, which I feared was a precursor of things to come. I trained hard in preparation for this, but if there was one thing I hadn't devoted enough attention to, it was hill work. It didn't take long for me to realize they were going to give me trouble.

Not far down the road, iTunes shuffled to a song called *Run* by the band Collective Soul. When I heard the line, "Have I got a long way to run" I shook my head and laughed a nervous laugh. I do have a *long way* to run. And thank you iTunes for pointing that out, as though I needed any more reminders of what I'm up against.

In the early afternoon, Google Maps' walking route guided me onto Coastal Route 1 (my run may be of my own making, but I'm letting Google Maps work out the details). I soon developed a strategy for tackling hills. Well it wasn't as much a strategy as a reward system. Ascending a hill, I would take a highly-coveted (and deserved) break, which included guardrail lounging.

Running The Coast For A Cure

Now, if you don't know what "guardrail lounging" is, that's because I'm making this up as I go. Basically, it consists of sipping on water from my hydration pack and chomping on chocolate covered energy bars, which, at that point, were warm and gooey.

Although the hills were tough, my surroundings were beautiful. Undeveloped woodland dominated the terrain. And, every so often, between the trees I could see the sundrenched waters of brooks and streams. The beauty of the area made those miles rather enjoyable (well, as enjoyable as can be when you're running by yourself on the first day of a three-month long trek).

A bit past the 18-mile mark, I came upon a church, which in this rural area made for a good landmark and called it a day. Despite my pre-run jitters (and my "during-the-run" jitters), I was pleased with my performance – 18.5 miles. It was a great start, and it was great to have Day 1 in the books.

My new friend Vicki Kilton picked me up and drove me to The Riverside Inn, where I'm staying while I'm in the area. Vicki is an employee at the inn and agreed to drop me off at my starting point and pick me up at my ending point for the first few days. Being alone and without a dedicated driver, finding Vicki was a godsend.

Now, you're probably wondering who in their right mind would set out on a run of this magnitude without a support vehicle and without the certainty of rides. Well, the plan was for an old friend of mine (who shall remain nameless) to do the driving and provide support. However, a last minute "cancellation" has left me

Al DeCesaris

fending for myself. Nothing like adding pressure to an already pressure-packed situation.

That evening, I had dinner at Cohill's in Lubec. While sitting at the bar eating a lobster dish (you don't come all the way to Maine and not try the lobster), I spoke with fellow customer, Mary. After telling her about my run, we started chatting with bartender Glen and discovered that he (like myself) is from Annapolis, Maryland. What are the odds there would be another person from Annapolis in this sleepy little town and that we'd meet the one day I was there? Had I not told Mary and Glen about my efforts, we never would have made that connection, and they never would have learned about the cause I'm running for. It reaffirmed the importance of speaking out – and, in this case, speaking *up* – for what you believe in. For me, this run is the means by which I can do that to raise awareness and funds for Sturge-Weber syndrome research and help further the efforts to find a cure for this devastating disorder. And, with each mile I run, I'll deliver that message loud and clear.

Day 2 (9/9/14): Whiting, ME to Whitneyville, ME [15.7 miles]

Rocky, the innkeeper and chef at The Riverside Inn, started my day off right with a healthy breakfast of fresh fruit, scrambled eggs, and a heaping portion of bacon. Okay, so maybe it wasn't *completely* healthy. Before I finished, Rocky pulled out a map and showed me what the road ahead had in store for me – lots of twists and turns and more hills. Judging from the look on Rocky's face, he was either doubtful that I could do this or concerned for my safety, maybe both.

As I walked back to my room I wondered, *am I crazy to have taken this on? Am I in over my head?* Of course, I knew the answer to both questions was yes. You have to be a little crazy to take on an endeavor like this. But, the more pertinent question is – do I doubt I can do this? The answer to that is a resounding no. Whether misguided or not, I truly believe I can do this.

Later that morning, Vicki, with her adorable two-year-old granddaughter in tow, picked me up and drove me to the church where I left off yesterday. I don't think Vicki understood why I needed to get back to that exact spot. I get that. It's not like I'm in a race or trying to set a record. Still, it's important to me that I cover every mile (every foot actually). Jenna and all those living with Sturge-Weber syndrome get no shortcuts, neither will I.

From the beginning of the day's run, I had to deal with the hills Rocky warned me about. Aside from slowing me down, they caused intermittent discomfort in my right ankle. Whenever it flared up, I made sure to check my form and slow my pace. More often than not, I realized my form had broken down – my shoulders and arms would be tensed up, I'd be slouched over, I'd be over-extending my stride, or any number of other common mistakes. Fatigue was the usual culprit. I'd then make the necessary adjustments and the discomfort would subside. But the more fatigued I got, the more my form broke down. Before long, I was running (lumbering to be accurate) down the road, repeating the words "watch your form, mind your pace" over and over.

In addition to the ankle discomfort, I had to deal with a narrow, uneven shoulder of cracked and crumbling pavement. It had me jumping and sidestepping potholes and chunks of broken asphalt. When I saw no cars coming, I stepped onto the roadway and ran on the white line since it provided a flat surface and, surprisingly, a little cushion. To my disappointment, it never seemed to last. Even though this part of Maine is sparsely populated, Route 1 through this area is busy. As a result, I spent the majority of my time navigating the "obstacle course" of a shoulder at a slow pace.

Around noon, I reached Machias, the site of the first naval battle of the American Revolution. After passing

Running The Coast For A Cure

the shops and restaurants in the heart of town, I crossed the Machias River. The bridge over it had a great view of the river's Bad Little Falls. Even though they were little, they were rocky and rough (I suppose that's where "Bad" comes into play).

That afternoon, my left knee started to bother me. Like before, I recited the words "watch your form, mind your pace" and performed my "maintenance check." My pace was fine, but my form was a mess. The corrective measures included engaging my core, straightening my torso, stabilizing my hips, relaxing my shoulders, and shortening my stride. I'm not sure which of those helped, but the discomfort subsided. Still, the thought that I might be developing a knee injury had me concerned.

About an hour later, Vicki came to get me. Although I would have liked to put in another hour, it was good that she came when she did. My knee and ankle were in serious need of ice … as was the rest of my body.

That evening I went to Skywalker's Bar and Grille in Machias. While eating, I had the good fortune of being waited on by Sara, an affable southern gal from North Carolina. Her southern hospitality, like her southern accent, was apparent. Even though she had other customers to attend, Sara was nice enough to let me tell her about Jenna and my run. She then offered to share our Facebook page with her friends and even fixed me up with a bag of ice for my sore knee. After running roughly 34 miles in two days on hilly terrain, that was one of the nicest things anyone could have done for me.

Day 3 (9/10/14): Whitneyville, ME to Columbia, ME [16 miles]

Months before setting out, I spoke to several accomplished ultra-runners to find out what to expect and how to prepare. One was Ray Zahab, a former pack-a-day smoker, who ran over 4,300 miles across the Sahara Desert and has since accomplished many other amazing athletic feats. Another was Helene Neville, a cancer survivor, who ran over 2,500 miles from California to Florida and, for an encore, ran down the West Coast and up the East Coast. Both Ray and Helene shared their insight and offered advice. To accomplish my goal, I learned that I need to be prepared, be smart, and believe in myself.

Well, I made great efforts to prepare myself. Within weeks of completing my cross-country bike ride, the training began, as did my research on long-distance running. And, as I did when I cycled across America, I believe I can do this. Still, other things need to come together for me to succeed, things I can't fully control. The biggest of which is staying injury free.

Unlike cycling, which is a controlled motion, running is a high impact activity. Minute after minute, hour after hour, day after day, I'm subjecting my body to constant pounding. Since I don't have much experience, I'll have

Al DeCesaris

to use the knowledge I've gained to minimize the risks of injury. Today, discomforts in my right ankle and left knee tell me I should play it safe. Thus, I've decided to dial back the number of miles I was planning to cover each day until I have a few weeks under my belt.

Although it was great running weather (high 60s and sunny), the run was difficult. Not far into it, my ankle discomfort turned to pain. I tried to mitigate the problem by correcting my form and slowing my pace, but the pain didn't subside. After several frustrating miles, I employed the "power-walker" approach. Yet, even that didn't alleviate the pain. So, I slowed my pace even more and employed what could best be described as the "zombie shuffle." It helped reduce the pain, though I should have just walked. I would have been moving faster.

At least I had picturesque scenery to preoccupy me. As I plodded along, I passed several little waterways and blueberry fields. As I've experienced from the blueberry juice and blueberry bread I've had since I've been in the area, if you're a fan of the sweet yet tart indigo (er ... *blue*) berry, look no further; "Downeast" Maine, as this area is affectionately referred to by the locals, is where it's at.

The day's run ended at a restaurant on Route 1 in Columbia. Again, Vicki picked me up and drove me back to the Riverside Inn. Since I had made it a good distance past the inn, it was time for me to move on to accommodations farther down the road. As I said my goodbyes to Vicki (this kind-hearted woman's help cannot be overstated), Rocky and his wife Ellen came out to see me off. To my surprise, the couple presented me with a donation for the cause. I later learned that Vicki had donated a portion of her driving time as well. The generosity of my new friends was amazing.

I then drove to the Englishman's Bed and Breakfast, a charming B&B on the banks of Narraguagus River in Cherryfield. The owners, Kathy and Peter, greeted me warmly when I arrived and helped me get settled in. Blueberry scones and a bag of ice for my ankle hastened the process.

Before calling it a night, I called Bryan Springer, one of my best friends from high school and a key member of my medical team. Bryan is an Orthopedic Surgeon as well as an avid runner. If anyone knows how to treat an ankle injury, it's Bryan. He recommended treatments I could self-administer − rest, ice, compression, and elevation − and prescribed an anti-inflammatory. He then advised that during my runs, when I need a break, I should try my best to keep moving rather than coming to a complete stop. That way I'll stay loose and still cover my miles. He also recommended that I make a conscious effort to incorporate some walking into my day, especially on steep hills.

Well, tomorrow is a new day. I hope − by following doctor's orders − it will bring a pain-free run, or at least a tolerable one.

Day 4 (9/11/14): Columbia, ME to Gouldsboro, ME [18.9 miles]

My day began with an egg and ham casserole … actually, two egg and ham casseroles. (It seems my appetite is growing.) While I ate, I chatted with a few of the other guests at the B&B, Bonnie from Maine and Anita and Blaine from Nova Scotia. I told them all about my run (the three painful and tiring days I've experienced thus far). They were supportive of my efforts and interested to learn about Sturge-Weber syndrome. When I headed out, they wished me well and said they'd follow my journey through our website.

Peter, the Englishman of the Englishman's Bed and Breakfast, then drove me to the restaurant in Columbia where I left off yesterday. As we made our way there, we formulated a plan for meeting up later in the day (or, more accurately, a plan for how Peter would find me as I hoofed it down the road). There was a forecast of afternoon showers, so we decided to "meet up" around 1:30pm … somewhere along Route 1.

It was a bit chillier than I expected and the wind, which hadn't been a factor thus far, was gusting. Yet, it didn't matter because the pain I felt yesterday in my right ankle was all but gone, and my legs felt good (not

Al DeCesaris

like the sore and weary ones I've had nearly every waking minute since the journey began).

Even so, I made sure to follow Bryan's advice about walking the steep hills and moving through my breaks. I also followed a recommendation my sister made about periodically crossing to the other side of the road and running *with* traffic. Now, I realize this isn't the safest thing to do. (When you're running on the road, you're supposed to run *against* traffic so you can see vehicles coming toward you.) But, when the shoulders of the road have downward slopes, switching it up every so often helps reduce the stress on the body from having to compensate for the uneven surface.

For the first time since I set out, I wore compression sleeves on my calves. They're said to provide a number of benefits including supporting and stabilizing muscles, reducing swelling and inflammation, and increasing blood flow. Well, whatever I owe the credit to, today I noticed a big difference. I felt lighter and quicker.

Another thing working in my favor was I didn't have as many hills to deal with today. Not to say there weren't a few big ones, but there were far less than I'd encountered in previous days. One section of road, however, presented a problem. After leaving Route 1 for Route 1A (I was told that taking the alternate route would shave a few miles off my run), I came upon a freshly-paved section of road that had no shoulder. It was also windy and hilly, making it difficult to see vehicles coming around the bends. This led to nervous walking on the hills and tense running on the flats. After

Running The Coast For A Cure

a while, the road leveled and straightened out and the shoulder reemerged. This was a boon to my safety ... and my soaring blood pressure.

Later in the day, I crossed the Narraguagus River. (Yep, the same one the B&B is located on.) Too bad my route didn't take me past the B&B itself; if it had, I could have saved Peter a trip.

Just past the river, I merged back onto Route 1 in Milbridge. Although I was in and out of the town in under 15 minutes, it was wonderful to see people and to see life. With the exception of a few occasions, since I began the run, my days have been spent in remote areas. I often go hours on end without seeing a soul. Of course, I knew it'd be like this, but I had no idea just how isolated and alone I'd feel. I guess that's why I was so excited when I ran through Milbridge. Just seeing a few smiling faces lifted my spirits and boosted my energy.

For the next several hours I made great time. Around 1pm, I reached the county line. Crossing from Washington County into Hancock County filled me with a sense of accomplishment. Now I realize it wasn't like climbing Mount Everest, but I had just run across a county ... and a big one at that.

Not long after, I came upon Linwood's, an eclectic little concert venue within the town limits of Gouldsboro. I then spotted Peter's car, and not a minute too soon. As he pulled over to pick me up, the rain started falling.

While yesterday was all business, today was kind of fun, and pain-free to boot. For the first time since I set out, I felt like I was hitting my stride.

Day 5 (9/12/14): Gouldsboro, ME to Ellsworth, ME [20.8 miles]

After packing my things and inhaling a hearty breakfast of Belgium waffles, eggs, and the local drink of choice – blueberry juice, Kathy and Peter presented me with a discount on my stay. It was their way of contributing to the cause. Kathy also gave me a sign she made for me should I have trouble finding a ride back to where I finished my run yesterday; one I hoped I wouldn't need to use.

The plan for the day was to run 20+ miles along Route 1 from Gouldsboro to Ellsworth. My family booked a room for me in Ellsworth at the Eagle's Lodge Motel, just off of Route 1; that way I could run right to my motel and wouldn't need a ride at the end of the day. It sounded good in theory – I just needed to find a ride back to Linwood's in Gouldsboro so I could get started.

When I arrived at the Eagle's Lodge Motel there was no one there who could give me a lift and no taxis available. How did I not see that coming? So, I strapped on my hydration pack, laced up my shoes, and broke out the sign Kathy made for me, which read, "I need a ride to Route 1 in Gouldsboro to start my charity run." And for the first time in my life, I set out to hitch a ride.

Al DeCesaris

From what I've been told, hitchhiking in Maine is commonplace. Even so, I was nervous about doing it. I wanted to get publicity for the run, but not by ending up in the *Missing Persons* section of the newspaper.

After 15 minutes of holding my thumb – and Kathy's sign – in the air, two guys pulled over and gestured for me to hop in. As soon as I got in and got a good look at them, I regretted doing this. These roughnecks had beer in the front seat and looked as though they were either still partying from last night or had gotten an early start on tonight's festivities. I had no idea if they were going to give me a ride or drag me into the woods and leave me for dead.

After covering the basics (namely, why anyone in their right mind would bum a ride to a random location some 20 miles down the road only to run those same 20 miles back to where he started), I learned that their names were Conrad and Liam and that Conrad is the owner-operator of a local granite company. I also learned that Conrad donated the granite used in the *Rock of Angels* memorial dedicated to the victims of the Sandy Hook School shooting. I was blown away by his kindness and generosity. I guess the old adage "you can't judge a book by its cover" has real merit.

Although Conrad and Liam were unable to give me a ride all the way to Gouldsboro (they had to get back to work), they were good enough to get me halfway there. They even offered me a cold beer for the road. Had they offered it at the end of the day's run rather than the beginning, I would have taken them up on the offer.

Running The Coast For A Cure

I then took up position on the side of the road with Kathy's sign again in hand. Ride number two came not long after. Jared and Mandy were my "chauffeurs" this time. As we traveled, I told them about Jenna and the cause. I do my best to explain why I'm running to the people I meet. In some ways that's as important as the running itself. Even though I was leery about hitchhiking, it proved (at least on this day) well worth it. It gave me the opportunity to educate four people about Sturge-Weber syndrome and taught me a valuable lesson too.

At Linwood's I met Lenny, the owner, and a cyclist named John, who was on the final leg of a cross-country bicycle ride. The three of us were soon joined by Phil, one of Lenny's friends. Like Lenny, Phil was surprised to discover that two adventurers had converged on Linwood's at the same time. John and I shared stories of our journeys before heading our separate ways – John north on Route 1 toward Lubec and me south on Route 1 toward Key Largo.

After getting started, I developed discomfort in my right heel. I hadn't felt anything like this before, and it had me worried. Then again, these days pretty much every little ache and pain does. Yet, rather than letting fear take hold, I chalked it up to the fact that the Newton Gravity III running shoes I was wearing (I've been rotating three different types of shoes since I set out) were worn and in need of replacement. I'd put some serious miles on them during my training runs this summer and should have replaced them weeks ago. At least that's what I told myself....

Al DeCesaris

Helping distract me from the discomfort in my heel were breathtaking views of ponds, bays, harbors, and coves surrounded by forested land and low mountains. Also helping, the crisp, cool air had a distinct scent of pine. (They don't call it "The Pine Tree State" for nothing.) Every so often, I could smell a hint of burning wood from a nearby chimney as well. My days may be long and difficult, but my surroundings make them manageable and often times enjoyable.

Later that afternoon, I reached Ellsworth and arrived at my motel soon after. Once settled in, I called my friend John Wall to let him know how I was feeling. John is an ER doctor and part of the medical team that's advising me, just as they did when I cycled across America. Based on my symptoms, John recommended the go-to treatments for running injuries – rest, ice, compression, and elevation. I then asked what had become the burning question – How long can I go before I need to take a day off? In short, he told me as long as I feel good, I don't need to take a day off. *So, if I'm feeling good, I can run down the entire East Coast without taking a day off?* I surmised, then laughed myself back to reality. What John was actually saying is I need to listen to my body. Well, I'm only about 90 miles in and I've already had pain and discomfort in my right ankle, left knee, and right heel … I think it's safe to say, my body is trying to tell me something.

Day 6 (9/13/14): Ellsworth, ME to Bucksport, ME [20.1 miles]

I slept in this morning to give my body extra recovery time. After the week I had, it needed it. When I finally got out of bed, I was surprised to notice that my right heel felt good. Well, good enough to give it a go. Still, I wasn't sold it would hold up the entire day, so I taped it and put on an extra pair of socks for added cushion.

After foam-rolling my legs (which in medical terms is known as self-myofascial release and in actual terms is known as self-inflicted torture) and stretching (both of which are part of my pre-run routine), I set out at a gingerly pace. Although I tend to start my runs off slowly, with my heel being a concern, today I *really* wanted to ease into it. It was a good thing too because about a quarter of a mile down the road a woman pulled out of a parking lot without looking. The approaching car sent my heart racing and my legs into action. I'm not sure how I did it, but I managed to maneuver my body out of the way just in time. A second later I would have ended up roadkill or, at the very least, with a severe limp. The woman was down the road and out of sight before I even processed what had happened. *What the hell! Does she realize she almost hit me?* I wondered with both shock and anger.

Al DeCesaris

Although I got right back to the run, it took some time to calm my nerves. It didn't help that this area was overrun with strip malls and shopping centers and had cars and trucks darting this way and that. Those first few miles were stressful ones.

After passing through Ellsworth's historic downtown, I came to a serene stretch of Route 1 that runs between low rock walls topped with pines and a variety of other trees, the leaves of which looked as though they were ready to turn. Not far beyond that, I was treated to a spectacular view of a large pond surrounded by dense woodland. The scenery helped me get my mind off the scare of my "near-demise."

Despite the respite, it seems no day in this part of Maine is complete without having to face at least a few big hills. I made sure to follow doctor's orders and walked them. The more manageable ones I shuffled up and down and was pleased my heel held up well.

Later in the day, the sky grew dark and had the look of rain. Although I knew I wouldn't melt if I got wet (I *was* already drenched with sweat), I didn't want to get caught in the rain on unfamiliar roads. I needed to see where I was going ... and I needed the cars and trucks to be able to see me. So, I picked up the pace and tried my best to get to my destination before the sky opened up on me. Over the next couple of hours, I made great time and was able to reach the McDonald's in Bucksport well before dark and well before the rain started falling.

When I set out this morning, I wasn't sure what the day would bring. Judging by the way I felt yesterday, I

Running The Coast For A Cure

feared I might have done serious damage to my foot. Yet, I moved well today both with running and with dodging cars. The only catch was, I was staying a second night at the motel in Ellsworth and needed to get back there. So, I did what you do when you need a ride in Maine – I put my thumb in the air and hitched one.

After a few curious stares (I'm sure the fact that I was dripping with sweat wasn't helping convince anyone to let me in their car), a young woman named Rebecca pulled over and offered me a ride. After I told her about my run, she brought up a number of different topics (each more or less at the same time). It was hard keeping up with her. Yet, during the course of our talk (er … *her* talk), I gained unique insight into Maine as well as a bunch of other random topics. Before dropping me off, she showed me a beautiful waterfront parcel of land covered with blueberry fields and surrounded by pine trees. It was quintessential Maine. The scene just needed a lighthouse and a lobster to round things out.

That evening I had the good fortune of visiting the seaside town of Bar Harbor with Sara, whom I met in Machias. True to form, the southern belle extended her southern hospitality by showing me the town. Bar Harbor is a popular tourist destination, and over the years has been home to many prominent people. I could see why – cafes, restaurants, and shops lined the streets and yachts filled the harbor. As I walked the streets (at a slow, careful pace), I thought Bar Harbor alone warranted a trip back to Maine. Although next time I'll be driving through Maine, not running.

Day 7 (9/14/14): Bucksport, ME to Belfast, ME [16.9 miles]

After breakfast, I donned my running attire, packed my things, and drove to the McDonald's in Bucksport where I left off yesterday. The plan was to leave my car there and have Mike Carignan from the Knights of Columbus drive it to the hotel in Belfast where I'm staying tonight. My father had reached out to the Knights for assistance, and Grand Knight Carignan answered the call, literally and figuratively.

Under normal circumstances, turning my car over to a complete stranger would have seemed absurd to me. Yet, this is Maine and over the past week I've been bumming rides and even hitchhiking without any trouble. So, in a lot of ways, this seemed routine to me.

As soon as I got out of my car, I realized that the run today was going to be a very chilly and windy one. *What the heck happened to summer?* I wondered. Although it is still technically summer, I think it's safe to say that summer, at least in this part of Maine, is all but finished.

About a mile down the road, Mike Carignan spotted me as I approached the bridge over the Eastern Channel and pulled over to get my car key from me. Although we had never met, I don't think Mike had any trouble identifying me. I'm fairly certain I'm the only

Al DeCesaris

person in the entire state running down Route 1 in patriotic red, white, and blue running apparel. Mike greeted me like an old friend and put my misgivings (the few that I had) to rest. After chatting a bit, Mike saw me off with a big smile and words of encouragement.

As I crossed the channel, I reflected on how kind it is of this man, who knows next to nothing about me, to go out of his way to help. And it's not just Mike. After he drives my car to the hotel in Belfast, his wife Mary is going to pick him up and bring him back to his car. And they're going to do this for the next several days without recognition and without payment. It's the kind of thing that restores your faith in humanity.

A mile or so farther, I came to the Penobscot Narrows Bridge. It's a 2,120-feet cable-stayed bridge with an observation tower (the first of its kind in the United States) and fantastic views of the Penobscot River and Bucksport in the distance.

Just past the bridge, Route 1 curled to the left under a tall rock wall of various hues of gray, brown, and tan flecked with a ruddy copper tone. Atop the wall were trees with leaves of myriad shades of green and others revealing the first hints of autumn. It was a captivating sight and unlike anything I had seen thus far.

Later in the day, I started to develop discomfort and pain in the inside portion of my lower right leg. It wasn't terrible, but it was yet another thing I had to deal with ... and worry about. Fortunately for me, over the next several hours I had amazing views of Long Cove, Searsport Harbor, and Belfast Bay to keep my mind off

Running The Coast For A Cure

the discomfort. Without a doubt, Maine has no shortage of spectacular water views.

As I approached Belfast, fatigue started to set in. With each step, my legs seemed to get heavier and heavier, making the last few miles arduous. However, I did get a boost when I caught sight of my hotel – the Belfast Harbor Inn and my car in the parking lot, *intact*. (Mike and Mary had come through. Truth be told, there was never any doubt.) The fact that the inn had a phenomenal view of Belfast Bay was an added bonus.

That evening I enjoyed a relaxing meal in a restaurant next door to the hotel. While eating my dinner (and an entire basket of bread), I reflected on how I had just completed the first week of my run and logged roughly 127 miles. That's an average of about 18 miles per day. It was a good start. However, I knew if I was to reach Key Largo in the 90 to 100 days that I projected the journey would take, I need to increase my average a bit. Otherwise, I'll be celebrating Christmas in my running shoes on the side of Route 1.

Day 8 (9/15/14): Belfast, ME to Camden, ME [20.6 miles]

When I woke up this morning I saw I had an email from a TV station (FOX 22/ABC 7) that wanted to interview me about the run. *Great news!* News coverage will help us reach a wider audience with our message.

An hour into my run, I received a call from reporter Patrick Thomas. He was on his way to meet me and needed to know where I was. You would think, knowing that someone was coming to interview me, I would have been keeping track of my whereabouts; but I didn't have a clue. I had just run past a church, though I didn't catch the name of it … and it stood atop a big hill. I hated the thought of having to run back up it, but I needed a landmark for Patrick to find me. So, up the hill I went.

Thankfully, the name of the church was enough for Patrick to track me down. Before long, he and I were standing on the side of the road going over the plan. Basically, he was going to film me running down the road from different vantage points, and afterward interview me. It seemed simple enough, at least for me. I was running down this road anyway.

After Patrick gave me the green light, I put in my earbuds, cranked up the music, and started off. What I thought was going to be a few shots of me running toward and away from the camera turned out to be a lengthy filming session. After capturing each shot, Patrick loaded his gear into his car, drove ahead, then set up his camera again to catch the next shot. He must have done this at least a half dozen times. After we were both good and tired, Patrick interviewed me.

As we were wrapping things up, Mary and Mike Carignan pulled up to say hello. They were transporting my car from Belfast to the inn I'm staying at tonight in Camden. The timing of their visit couldn't have been better. Patrick thought it'd be great to have a local resident like Mike explain how he'd gotten involved with my run and what he was doing to help. What a fantastic way to recognize all of Mike's efforts. Before they started the interview, I said my goodbyes to Patrick and the Carignans and continued down the road.

I ran south on Route 1 along Penobscot Bay and enjoyed spectacular water views. It was one postcard-esque scene after the other. Yet, there were also a couple of steep climbs that were downright torturous, reminding me just how demanding this run can be.

Around 3:30pm, I reached Camden, a charming seaside community. Route 1 runs through the heart of town past Camden Harbor and a number of high-end restaurants and upscale shops. I slowed my pace and delighted in the sights, sounds, and smells – souvenirs in shop windows, conversations of passersby, and delectable aromas wafting from restaurants.

Soon after, I reached the Hartstone Inn, a beautifully restored Mansard-style Victorian home, where my family

Running The Coast For A Cure

booked a room for me. My first thought was, *there must be a mistake. This place has to be outside of our budget.* But, as I later learned, my father told the inn's staff about my run and they offered a reduced rate, making a night at the Hartstone Inn the cheapest and best option in Camden. It appears suffering through 20+ miles on foot comes with a few perks.

Another bonus was the Hartstone had a spa across the street. After showering, I headed over for a massage. Masseuse DeAnna (AKA the world's biggest Seattle Seahawks fan) took the time to put my legs and feet back in working order. I don't know what was more unbelievable, how incredible I felt after the massage or the fact that DeAnna and her husband had said their vows in a Seahawks-themed wedding, complete with Seahawks jerseys, a Seahawks wedding cake, a football turf aisle, and a goalpost atop the altar.

That night my older brother Joe called to see how everything was going. After getting him up to speed, he asked the big question on his mind (and just about everyone else's), "Is the run harder than the bike ride?" At the time I did it, my cross-country bike ride was the hardest thing I'd ever done. Yet, from the little I've experienced thus far, this is even more challenging, and not just physically. It's mentally more challenging too. But what really sets it apart from the ride is the wear and tear on my body. At the end of each day (and often during them), I feel like I've been fed through a meat grinder – chewed up and spit out. So yeah, the run is harder than the ride … much, *much* harder.

37

Day 9 (9/16/14): Camden, ME to Waldoboro, ME [18.1 miles]

A rainy morning gave me an excuse to sleep in and enjoy some leisure time, which I took full advantage of. Once I'd done a quality job of both the sleeping and the "leisuring," I packed my things and bid the Hartstone Inn adieu (that's the fancy way of saying goodbye when you're staying in a fancy establishment).

I then drove to the not-so-fancy Moody's Motel in Waldoboro where I'm staying tonight. The motel is located right off of Route 1 about 18 miles southwest of Camden. When I arrived, I met Debbie, the manager, and two of her young grandchildren (evidently, managing Moody's is a family affair). Debbie had a keen interest in what I'm doing and wanted to know about Sturge-Weber syndrome. Whenever someone shows interest, I make sure to tell them all about the disorder and how it affects Jenna ... and sometimes I tell them about it even if they don't show interest.

After explaining that I needed to get back to Camden to begin the day's run, Debbie went out of her way to see if any of her employees could help. A woman named Jody agreed to drive me, and Debbie arranged to have her work covered. It might not have a spa like the Hartstone, but Moody's was winning me over.

Al DeCesaris

On our way to Camden, Jody told me all about Moody's Motel as well as Moody's Diner, which is just down the road from the motel. I'd never heard of Moody's Diner, but apparently it is quite famous. As the story goes, it has been around for over 80 years and has been featured in magazines and television programs time and again. After learning of its storied history, I figured I'd be a fool not to try it and decided that tonight I'd be eating dinner at Moody's.

When I started, the heavy rains of earlier were little more than an intermittent drizzle. An hour or so later, even that came to an end. However, the sky remained overcast making for uninspiring running conditions.

In the afternoon, I received a call from one of my good friends from college, Chris Conte. He's been an ardent supporter of my efforts and wanted to see how I was doing. During our conversation, I learned he'd just suffered a stress fracture in his foot while training for the Chicago marathon. The news was disheartening. I knew he'd been training for quite some time and had been taking all the necessary precautions. It seems no matter how careful you are, sometimes injuries just happen.

As for me, prior to creating my "For A Cure" charity events, I never imagined I'd be able to run these many miles each day, much less do it day in and day out. (Now, I do realize this wouldn't be possible without Jenna inspiring me nor without the support and encouragement of a great number of people.) Yet, if I'm to make it all the way to Key Largo, I'll need to remain injury free, or at least keep the injuries to a minimum.

Running The Coast For A Cure

I know this will be no easy feat. I not only have overuse injuries to worry about, but I also have the random turn of an ankle and an infinite number of other freak injuries to stress over. Oh, and what about the vehicles whizzing by me all day long? Even a glancing blow from a compact car would be disastrous. The threat of a run-ending injury loomed over me with every step I took.

In spite of my worries, the rest of the day was uneventful, which was a good thing in light of Chris' injury news. When I got back to Moody's Motel, I met Debbie's husband Bob, who is a preacher at a local church. After learning of my run, Bob said to me, "and let us run with perseverance the race marked out for us." It was a bible passage (Hebrews 12:1-3), and a fitting one at that. I shared with him my concerns about getting injured. Bob listened with patience and compassion, then spoke to me about letting go of fear and putting my trust in the Lord.

That evening as I sat in Moody's Diner and ate not one meal but two (as I said before, my appetite is growing), I thought about what preacher Bob had said. Whether my body holds up till the end or I develop a significant injury like Chris did, worrying about it isn't going to help one bit. I trained hard, I did my homework, I'm consulting with medical professionals, and I'm being as safe as I can. In the end, that's all I can do. Beyond that, things are out of my control. Whatever the Lord's plan is, I need to trust in Him and have faith.

41

Day 10 (9/17/14): Waldoboro, ME to Wiscasset, ME [18.3 miles]

In the morning I drove to the Newkirk Inn, a beautiful 1870s Greek Revival B&B, located in downtown Wiscasset. Upon my arrival, the innkeeper, Chris, and his Miniature Dachshund, Gunther, greeted me warmly. Knowing that I'm doing a charity run, Chris gave me a discount on a standard room, then upgraded me to one of the suites. He even offered to drive me back to Moody's, saving me the trouble of having to hunt for a ride. This whole situation with having to find and coordinate rides has been one of the most mentally challenging aspects of the run. Dare I say, it's almost as difficult to deal with as the run itself. (Mental note: next time I do a 2,000-some-odd mile charity run, make sure I have a dedicated driver. Now accepting applications!)

I was blown away by Chris' kindness and generosity. Yet, as you know, it isn't exclusive to just him. Since Day 1, people have been going out of their way to help me and support the cause: be it with rides, discounts, donations, advice, and encouragement. It's amazing the way the people of Maine have opened their hearts to me.

The day's run began with the biggest and steepest climb I've faced thus far. Although I would have loved to give it a go, I wasn't warmed up and was just starting what would be an 18+ mile day. So, I used my brains and not my brawn and took the hill at a careful pace.

Usually by mile three or four, I'm feeling limber and moving well, yet today that wasn't the case. Even after a couple of hours, I was stiff and tight. Making matters worse, it was warmer than it had been in days and I was sweating more than usual. The scant few times I was able to pick up the pace, my legs cramped up. Did I not drink enough water? Or maybe, after 10 straight days, my body had just had enough. Whatever the case, the miles *did not* come easy.

No matter how hard it gets, my problems don't compare to the struggles of those with Sturge-Weber syndrome. I was reminded of that when I learned from my family that Jenna needs to have another surgery on her right eye. Sturge-Weber syndrome caused the development of abnormal blood vessels on the right side of her face, behind her right eye, and on the surface of her brain. Although the abnormal blood vessels on her brain have led to her most serious problems – seizures and stroke-like episodes – those behind her eye caused glaucoma and have put her limited vision at serious risk.

From an early age, Jenna has had a number of surgical procedures on her right eye to reduce the eye's intraocular pressure. During one such procedure, she had an adverse reaction to the anesthesia and suffered a stroke-like episode, leaving her with significant weakness in her left arm and left leg, along with loss of motor coordination. Although she regained use of her

Running The Coast For A Cure

arm and leg, it was a precursor of things to come. Complications during subsequent surgical procedures caused other serious issues, including retina detachment and loss of vision. The thought of her having to undergo another such procedure had me very worried. It reinforced the significance of the run and how important it is that we continue to fight Sturge-Weber syndrome and work to find a cure.

A bit after 5pm, I came to the Sheepscot River and, with Wiscasset just beyond it, realized I was in the home stretch. I followed Route 1 onto Davis Island (it's a peninsula *actually*; they might want to re-think the whole "island" thing), then onto the bridge that crossed the river. Lucky for me, the bridge had a pedestrian only section, which kept me safe from speeding vehicles. It's not often I have my own area like that, so I took my time and enjoyed the spectacular water views.

When I got back to the Newkirk Inn, Chris reminded me about Red's Eats, which he'd recommended earlier. It's one of Maine's most famous seafood shacks, and its lobster roll has been voted #1 in the state several times.

Soon after, I was sitting at a picnic table out back of Red's enjoying an authentic Maine lobster roll. It was far and away the best lobster roll I have ever eaten. Yet this posed a real conundrum, Red's set the bar so darn high I don't think I'll ever be able to eat a lobster roll from anywhere else ever again.

Day 11 (9/18/14): Wiscasset, ME to Brunswick, ME [19.6 miles]

As I devoured an everything bagel with Taylor Ham and American cheese, I told Chris of my concerns about developing an injury. You'd have thought he knew I was going to bring up the subject because right away he mentioned a bible passage (Matthew 6:26-32) that would have made even Preacher Bob proud, "Can any one of you by worrying add a single hour to your life?" It reinforced what I'd been told and was now coming to understand, worrying about things doesn't help one bit.

After thanking Chris for his hospitality and support, I drove to the Americas Best Value Inn in Brunswick where I'm staying tonight. Upon my arrival, I met the owners, Anila and Harry. After I explained what I was doing, Anila agreed to drive me back to the Newkirk Inn so I could get the day's run started.

For the first few hours I made good time (at least by my standards). Of course, there were a few hiccups as there always are. At one point, iTunes sucked the life out of me when it shuffled to a song by James Taylor. (No offense to any James Taylor fans out there, but it's not exactly "get your heart pumping" kind of music). Not long after, iTunes shuffled to a Bon Jovi track, which, aside from giving me a boost, had me laughing (no

Al DeCesaris

offense to Bon Jovi fans either). I have diverse taste in music, so letting iTunes shuffle the songs keeps things unpredictable and entertaining, even when it's 70s folk singers and 80s hair-bands.

When I reached the city of Bath, Route 1 became congested and had me skirting around one high traffic area, then running in the grass along the shoulder-less stretch of another. Both situations were manageable, but they had me thinking, had I been cycling instead of running they would have caused major problems. This was the first time I realized that running has a distinct advantage over cycling. I made sure to make a mental note of it so when I find myself complaining about the difficulties of running, I remember to bite my tongue.

Later in the day, as I approached Brunswick, Route 1 opened up and turned into a busy highway. I had biked on the shoulder of a major interstate highway when I did my bike ride, so being on a busy road like this didn't bother me much. However, it must have bothered the police because a couple of miles in, a squad car pulled up behind me with its lights flashing and siren blaring. Before I knew what was happening, I was being "pulled over" (if that's what you call it) by one of Maine's finest.

Officer Steve pointed out that pedestrians are not allowed on this stretch of Route 1. Apparently, there were signs posted setting forth this restriction, though I didn't see them. He told me he'd drive me a few miles back to a place where I could get onto a parallel side road. The last thing I wanted to do was re-run miles. So, I explained to him how I have a GPS tracker on my

Running The Coast For A Cure

hydration pack and that people everywhere were tracking my movements through the GPS coordinates being displayed on our website and that I needed to maintain uninterrupted forward movement. Okay, so maybe I laid it on a bit thick, especially the "people everywhere were tracking my movements" part. It's more like a handful of people, the majority of whom are my immediate family. Still, it convinced Officer Steve to present me with another option – if I could get to the next exit, which was about two miles ahead, before he got a call, he'd let me continue on.

The catch was, if he did get a call before I reached the next exit, I'd have to get in the squad car, and he'd drop me off at the exit ... throwing my whole mileage tracking system into disarray. So, after already covering 12 miles, I sprinted two more while Officer Steve followed close behind. Keep in mind, when I say "sprinted" I'm talking about my version of full speed running, not Usain Bolt's. It's no secret, I'm not the fastest runner, even when my legs are fresh. I can only imagine what my "sprint" looked like after 11 straight days of running close to 20 miles a day. People driving by must have thought it was some crazy "low-speed chase." By the end of it, my eyes (from sweat) and legs (from fatigue) were burning. Yet, I did manage to make it to the exit before Officer Steve received a call ... and before I collapsed from exhaustion.

Before driving off, Officer Steve pointed out the pedestrian path that began by the exit and wished me well. After having a good laugh about the situation, I realized what I thought was cramping from my "record-setting sprint," wasn't cramping at all. It appeared I'd hurt my right shin. Something was wrong with my left ankle as well.

As I walked down the pedestrian path, discomfort turned to pain and pain to something awful. The last four miles back to the motel were a grueling endeavor, with lots of walking … and a little limping sprinkled in.

When I got to the motel, I decided to be proactive and filled the bathtub with cold water and ice. Long story short, my first ever attempt at an ice bath was an absolute disaster. I think the ice bath (all 45 seconds of it) might have been more painful than the injuries.

I called Bryan Springer to find out what I should do about the pain and swelling. He told me to rotate my ankle and shin in a bucket of ice water every 15 minutes. That wasn't what I wanted to hear, but the bucket was easier than the tub (that might have had something to do with which body parts I was submerging in the ice water) and did help reduce the swelling.

After suffering through the bucket of ice water for a couple of hours, I decided to call it a night. I went to bed wondering if the serious injury I'd been so concerned about had now befallen me.

Day 13 (9/20/14): Brunswick, ME to Falmouth, ME [19.4 miles]

I spent most of yesterday in my motel room resting and icing my swollen left ankle and right shin. I also spent it wondering if a day of rest would get me back on my feet or if I'd done serious damage. Whenever my thoughts gave in to despair like that, I reflected on the bible passage Chris shared with me and did my best to put the pointless worry out of my mind.

Aside from recovery time, the day off gave me the chance to buy a new pair of running shoes. The three pairs I brought with me – Brooks Glycerin, Asics Gel-Nimbus, Newton Gravity III – had considerable miles on them from the 11 days thus far and all my training runs this summer. After explaining the nature of my run and my current condition, the guys at the running store recommended the Hoka One One Stinson Lite. Hoka One Ones are extra cushiony and *extra big*. They kind of look like moon boots, but I'm not much into looks these days. It's all about comfort.

When I woke up this morning, I knew I should probably take another day off. But another day, or even another week, wouldn't be enough time to mend things if I'd done real damage. So, I decided I was going to do

Al DeCesaris

my best to reach the town of Falmouth, my destination for the day, even if I had to walk the entire way.

Bottom line, I'm striving to raise awareness and funds for Sturge-Weber syndrome research so a cure can be found. This run is just one way I'm doing that. So, whether I end up lame after one mile or run pain-free the rest of the way to Key Largo, I'm going to continue to fight this devastating disorder any way I can.

At breakfast, a woman came up to me and made a cash donation to the cause right on the spot. I was moved by her willingness to help, though I was a bit surprised – I hadn't even told her about my run. I soon learned that Anila was promoting it on my behalf. Since I arrived at their motel, Anila and Harry have been talking up my run to their guests and creating a real buzz. It was apparent the run was inspiring others to join the fight. This was yet another reason to keep pressing on.

After an extra-long session on my foam roller and lots of stretching, I put on my new Hokas and set out for what I hoped would be a 20-mile run. The first few miles I little more than shuffled my feet. But after I warmed up, I increased my pace and was surprised to discover that my left ankle held up well. In fact, I didn't feel any pain or discomfort in my ankle at all.

My right shin, however, was a different story. I had discomfort and subtle pain even when walking. Actually, it felt worse when I walked. Not that it felt great when I was running, but I did find that when I ran on the balls of my feet (AKA forefoot-striking) the pain wasn't as bad.

Running The Coast For A Cure

Unfortunately, I didn't know any tricks for tackling hills. Whether I ran or walked them, the pain was intense.

Towards the end of the day, my shin started throbbing something fierce. I made sure to watch (and correct) my form and mind (and slow) my pace. I even changed up my foot-strike, but nothing helped. As I hobbled along in pain, I wondered if my police-induced dash was responsible for my current condition. I also wondered if Officer Steve had meant to do me a favor by letting me run to the next exit ... or if he was just having a laugh at my expense.

The last few miles were brutal. I had to dig deep to stomach the pain. But then, out of nowhere, the pain subsided, and I was able to run unhampered. The respite only lasted a mile or two, but it left me with hope that I could manage this, and even push through it.

Around 5pm, I reached Falmouth and called it a day at McDonald on Route 1. It wasn't quite 20 miles, but all things considered I was happy with the miles I'd put in. A half hour later, Harry (driving my car as we arranged) pulled into the parking lot. As he started to get out of the driver's seat, I waved him off. I was too tired to drive.

By the time we reached his motel, I was feeling somewhat better and went inside to say my goodbyes. Anila wasn't there, though Harry assured me he would pass along my thanks to her. He wished me well and saw me off with an encouraging smile.

I then drove to the home of State Representative Janice Cooper. Janice had learned about my run from fellow Representative Katherine Cassidy and offered to host me for the night. It's remarkable, whenever I've needed help, kind and generous people have come to my aid.

After supplying me with my daily ration of ice, which helped ease the pain in my shin, Janice cooked a delicious dinner. The home-cooked meal was a welcome treat. I quickly cleaned my plate (had seconds and even started in on thirds), then retired to the guest room contented. Before calling it a night, I checked the weather for tomorrow and saw that it was supposed to rain. Although I didn't want to take another day off, some extra rest wouldn't hurt. I suppose I'll wait until tomorrow and let the weather … and my shin make the call.

Day 14 (9/21/14): Falmouth, ME to Biddeford, ME [20.8 miles]

I woke to falling rain, which was music to my ears. The more rain, the more rest. However, I didn't want to take the entire day off. As I've said before, if I don't stay on schedule, I'll be on the road well into the holidays, and I really don't want to be watching Ryan Seacrest ring in the New Year from a roadside motel. Actually, under no circumstances do I want to be watching Ryan Seacrest on New Year's Eve.

After a tall stack of blueberry pancakes, compliments of Janice, I put a call into Bryan Springer. Once I got him up to speed on my recent aches and pains, he determined that my right leg most likely has tibial stress syndrome, better known as shin splints. He told me it's quite common in runners, especially when the number of miles is increased significantly over a short period of time. Who knew? Well … I did. I guess I figured since I'd never had shin splints that I wouldn't get them now. Obviously, that wasn't the case.

Time off is the best remedy, Bryan advised. But, as you know, my time is limited. I didn't need to point that out to Bryan. He knows this. He also knows I'm not going to stop unless he tells me I must. So, not hearing any objections, I vowed to press on (and that included today).

After the rain let up, I followed Janice to Biddeford and parked my car at the Sleepy Hollow Motel, my destination for the day. I'm not sure how my family found this place, but I bet if they had seen it themselves, they never would have booked it. I've stayed in some seedy motels in my day, but this place ranks among the very worst. If the slummy exterior was any indication, it might be safer and more hygienic to sleep in my car. Speaking of the car, I prayed it'd be there when I got back.

After loading my hydration pack with PowerBars and GU Energy Gels, I hopped into Janice's car and we headed out. As we made our way to the McDonald's in Falmouth, Janice drove through Portland to show me the route I should take. She figured it would save me time and help me avoid confusion as I navigated the city. She obviously overestimated my short-term memory and my sense of direction. When we reached the Golden Arches, I thanked Janice and gave her a hug goodbye. Her hospitality was much appreciated.

During the early part of the run my right shin held up well and the pain was tolerable. Still, I made sure to avoid heel-striking as much as I could and went back and forth between forefoot and midfoot-striking. Of the three foot-strikes, heel-striking seems to cause the most pain, which stands to reason since it's known to produce the most injuries. The one benefit of having shin splints is that it might force me to break my bad habits and become a better runner.

Running The Coast For A Cure

Around 1:45pm, I reached the historic and picturesque seaside city of Portland. However, I couldn't find the road Janice recommended I take and missed out on running through the Old Port district along the harbor and past other sights of interest. It was disappointing because I was looking forward to checking it all out. It seems my "photographic memory" and "Magellan-like navigation skills" made things much more confusing and time consuming than they needed to be. Despite my best (or worst) efforts, I eventually got through the city and found my way back onto Route 1.

About 12 miles south of the city, I came upon an area with dense fog suspended above a vast and desolate marshland with cattails and tall grass swaying in the breeze. *Where the heck did this come from?* I had just run through the largest city in the state. The drastic change of scenery was shocking and quite surreal.

As the day wore on, my right shin started to bother me again. As though dealing with shin splints wasn't difficult enough, later in the day my right Achilles and right Soleus started to bother me too. I guess, by altering the way I normally run, I was putting stress on other parts of my leg that weren't conditioned to handle it.

With about five miles to go, I decided to pull in the reins before any more damage was done. As I walked, I got a call from one of my great college friends, Kevin Lewis (AKA Uncle Lew). I always enjoy my conversations with him because he's so upbeat and positive. If you ever need encouragement, Uncle Lew is

57

Al DeCesaris

your man. He's a cross between a football coach who gets his players so fired up they'd run through a brick wall for him and a motivational speaker who helps people achieve things they never believed possible. His enthusiasm and encouragement couldn't have come at a better time.

I arrived at the Sleepy Hollow just before dark. And, yes, my car was still there ... and no, it wasn't on cinderblocks. However, I began to panic when I saw the "Sorry We're Closed" sign out front and discovered that the door to the motel's reception area was locked. After several anxiety-filled phone calls, a woman turned on the lights and let me in. I'm not sure where she came from (who knows, maybe she was sleeping behind the front desk), but I was relieved to see her. I was also happy to be able to check into my room, even if it turned out to be the shabby and squalid establishment I presumed it to be ... which of course it was.

Day 15 (9/22/14): Biddeford, ME to North Berwick, ME [21.6 miles]

In the morning I drove to Angel of the Berwicks Bed & Breakfast in North Berwick, an impressive Victorian mansion built in the late 1800s by Mary Hobbs, one of the nation's first female industrialists. Ben, the current owner, greeted me when I arrived and showed me to my room, which I later learned was right across the hall from the room where the ghost of Mary Hobbs is seen on occasion. Apparently, she liked her house so much she decided to stay.

Ben drove me back to the Sleepy Hollow Motel. When he learned that I'd stayed there, he couldn't believe it. In all actuality, I still can't believe it. His reasoning however wasn't the same as mine. From what he told me, the night before I arrived two people were found dead in their motel room. To think I was worried about bed bugs and having my car stolen.

When I started the day's run, I felt energetic. It might have been a result of the astounding weather (mid 60s and sunny). There's nothing like a little sunshine to lift your spirits. Or it might have been because I was so excited to be putting some distance between myself and that macabre motel … though tonight I may have the ghost of Mary Hobbs to contend with.

As I made my way down Route 1, I was pleased to discover that my shin wasn't bothering me as much as it had been. However, I did have discomfort in my right ankle, the top of my right foot, and my right heel (pretty much everywhere from the ankle down). I guess I traded in my shin problems for a host of other problems.

Around midday, while running along a wooded area, I caught sight of something slithering underfoot and almost stepped on a snake. It was close, frighteningly close. Granted, the snake was only about a foot long, but the way I see it, a venomous snake bite is a venomous snake bite.

Later in the day, I had back-to-back encounters with unleashed dogs. The first looked like a family pooch that wanted to play with me. The second had the look of a wild beast that wanted to eat me. Lucky for me, dog number two was on the other side of a busy stretch of road. Otherwise, I might have had to break out the mace. Lord knows, I could not have outrun him.

Other than those brief encounters with my reptilian and canine friends, this stretch of Route 1 was tranquil. It was also scenic. On both sides of the road was woodland, and the leaves in the trees had just started to turn. I'd heard how spectacular New England's fall foliage can be, and how it draws people ("leaf peepers" as the locals refer to them) from near and far. Today, I was getting a preview of the rich palette of autumn colors these lands hold.

When I reached the town of Kennebunk (not to be confused with nearby Kennebunkport, the summer

Running The Coast For A Cure

home of former President George H.W. Bush), I turned off of Route 1 and onto SR 9A. I was to take this winding country road southwest about six miles, then get onto SR 9, another meandering country road, and follow that six miles or so to the B&B.

Just after 1:30pm, I reached an overpass that crosses Interstate 95. As I surveyed the straight, flat, and wide interstate below, I thought about how much easier things would be if I could take I-95 rather than these cumbersome country roads. However, pedestrians aren't permitted on interstates in Maine (or most states for that matter); so, for me it'll have to be the cumbersome country roads.

As the day wore on, my shin started hurting again. I did everything I could to mitigate the pain, yet nothing worked. About three miles from the B&B, the pain got so severe that I had to shut it down and walked the rest of the way.

Whether he had ill intent or not, this was Officer Steve's fault. This whole thing might come to an end because of him ... or so I told myself. I wanted to blame him, to blame someone or something for having developed this "rookie" injury. But the truth of the matter is – I *am* a rookie and probably would have developed shin splints at some point anyway. Regardless of what caused them, I need to take responsibility for my current predicament and focus my mental and physical energy on treating my injuries and getting my miles in.

Day 16 (9/23/14): North Berwick, ME to Lee, NH [20.4 miles]

The day started with a mouthwatering breakfast prepared by Sally, Ben's wife and co-owner of the Angels. While I ate, I enjoyed the company of three couples from Wisconsin, who I dubbed the "Wisconsin Six" (it was a lot easier than trying to remember all their names). They were a fun group and definitely had more fun last night than I did. No doubt, drinking cocktails by the B&B's backyard fire pit tops icing your legs and wincing in pain.

I set out soon after, thrilled to know I didn't have far to go before I reached "The Granite State" (that's New Hampshire for those not up to speed on their state nickname trivia). The excitement of crossing the state line made those last few miles in Maine seem easy.

Just before 2pm, I came to a bridge extending over the Salmon Falls River with a sign on it that read, "STATE LINE ROLLINGSFORD NEW HAMPSHIRE." I was ecstatic. Running through Maine was a major accomplishment, especially in light of the fact that I covered a lot of those miles on a bum leg. In truth, there were times over the past two weeks when I doubted whether I'd make it out of this never-ending state. As I stood there snapping one selfie after another to commemorate my achievement, I thought, *if my legs do give out on me, at least I'll have run through one state*.

Al DeCesaris at the New Hampshire state line.

I then came to another sign, this one welcoming travelers to New Hampshire and stating (in English and in French) the state's official motto: "Live Free or Die." The independence-centric phrase comes from a toast by General John Stark, the state's most famous soldier of the American Revolutionary War. "Live Free or Die: Death is not the worst of evils," were the words he wrote, expressing the sentiment of the Revolutionaries.

My excitement soon faded as the pain in my right shin grew. Over the next few miles, the pain became agonizing, and was even worse (if that's possible) on the downslopes. To my surprise, the strenuous climbs provided the only relief (albeit minimal), turning my view

Running The Coast For A Cure

of running hills on its head. Who'd have thought I'd be looking forward to the climbs and fearing the declines?

Around 3pm, as I passed through Dover, the pain in my shin became almost unbearable. *Did I have enough in me to make it to my destination before nightfall? ... to make it there at all?* Making matters worse, a couple of my toes started burning like they'd been set aflame; undoubtedly, the result of the blisters I'd been ignoring. With all of my other problems, treating blisters hadn't been a priority. Then, with one bad step, I heard something pop in my right shin. The pain should have shot off the charts, but it had been so intense for so long that I didn't notice any difference. *Whatever that was, maybe it'll improve things*, I thought against all reason.

Later in the day, out of nowhere, the pain subsided (how or why I haven't a clue) and I was able to get back to something that resembled proper running form. It was a pleasant surprise and reminded me just how much I enjoy running; when it doesn't hurt, it's actually fun. It's times like this that help me remember to be thankful for what I have, even if it's just a few pain-free minutes when I can pick up the pace.

When I reached Lee, I noticed a park to the side of the road and came to a stop there. A few minutes later, Ben pulled up in my car as we had arranged. Judging from the look on his face, he must have thought I was going to topple over. I kind of did too.

It was a difficult day, but it was also a good one. Actually, any day I reach my destination (be it by running, walking, or limping) is a good day.

When I got back to the B&B, I called John Wall to get his thoughts on my ailing shin. John informed me that if I did in fact have shin splints, they usually take four to six weeks to heal. That is, of course, if during that time you're resting your legs. The prognosis when you're covering 20 miles a day is uncertain.

Later, I called my parents to check in (i.e. let them know I'd survived another day). Before we got to talking, my dad passed the phone to Elizabeth Medlock, the mother of Sturge-Weber patient (an adorable six-year-old superhero aficionado), Liliana Mae (AKA Super Lily). She's an independent and determined little lady who knows more about Captain America, the Hulk, and Iron Man than the actors who play them on the big screen. Coincidentally, Elizabeth and Lily had flown to Maryland for an appointment with Dr. Anne Comi at the Kennedy Krieger Institute and were staying with my parents. Just as they had when I biked across America, Elizabeth and Lily are following my run and rooting me on.

"You better not quit!" was the first thing Elizabeth said to me. She went on to tell me how much this charity run means to her family and all the other families affected by Sturge-Weber syndrome. It meant the world to me to hear that. If that doesn't get me motivated to suck it up and get back out there, I don't know what will. So, pain or no pain, tomorrow I'll be putting in the miles and fighting for Jenna, Lily, and all those living with this devastating disorder with each and every step I take.

Day 17 (9/24/14): Lee, NH to Chester, NH [17.1 miles]

The day started with another entertaining breakfast with the Wisconsin Six. Although I missed out on the fire pit cocktail party a couple of nights back, over the past two days I got to spend time with my new friends and had some good laughs. They were a riot with their jokes and bantering, they were also caring and encouraging. Before they left, they informed me that they were going to make a donation to the cause and wished me well.

Not long after, I packed my things, loaded up my car, and said my goodbyes to Ben, Sally, and the Angel of the Berwicks. My stay at the stately old mansion was a nice one, even though I slept with one eye open and jumped at every little noise, fearing it was the ghost of Mary Hobbs. I'm happy to report: on my watch, there were no ghostly encounters.

I then drove to the Sleep Inn in Londonderry. My family chose the Sleep Inn because they were assured that someone from the hotel could help with rides. However, upon arrival I was told that there was no one available to assist me. I ended up sitting in the hotel lobby for the better part of an hour while the employees tried to come up with a solution. In the end, they found a

Al DeCesaris

car service that was able to drive me to the day's starting point, but valuable time had been lost.

When I met the driver, Lois, I realized that things had worked out for the best. She was sweet and wanted to know all about my run and the cause. It's so uplifting when strangers take a genuine interest in what I'm trying to accomplish and in the well-being of my niece.

When we reached the park where I left off and it was time to pay, Lois offered me a significant discount on the fare. She then assured me that she'd pick me up when I finished. It's positive encounters like this that make the adversity (and pain) of the run bearable.

Soon after getting started, I passed from the town of Lee into the town of Epping. Keep in mind, when I say "town" I'm using that term loosely. From what I've seen of New Hampshire, a town is often just a smattering of houses in the countryside with a gas station, church, or country store at its center.

While running through Epping, I somehow missed the turn I was supposed to take. I only went about 10 minutes out of my way, but it was frustrating to have to backtrack. It was ironic too because just this morning I told the Wisconsin Six that I never go backward. I guess I'll have to watch my use of the word "never."

I also need to be careful about making assertions without having all the facts. So, let me qualify this next statement by pointing out that I've only put in about 50 miles on the new Hoka One One Stinson Lites. Still, from what I've noticed so far, out of all the different running shoes I've been wearing, the Hokas are the

Running The Coast For A Cure

most comfortable of the bunch. The extra cushion really does make a difference. Granted, I didn't break any land speed records, but at least for the early part of the run I was in far less pain than I'd been in on previous days.

Later in the day, Google Maps' walking route led me down a deserted dirt road. I was skeptical at first, but I figured if Google Maps didn't know which way to go, who did? Yet, the "road" (I'm now using that term loosely too) turned into nothing more than a rugged trail that twisted and turned through dense woodland. Portions of it were washed out, forcing me to trudge through thick underbrush to stay dry. Also, trails shot off in various directions, which had me checking (and double checking) my location on Google Maps to make sure I was going the right way. I considered turning back, but I knew if I did, I'd lose considerable time. Still, I was just waiting for a bear or some other wild animal to pounce on me. My nerves (and my imagination) had me creeping along with my head on a swivel, a stick in one hand and mace in the other.

When I finally emerged from my off-road adventure, I was tired and wanted to take a break (and celebrate my survival). However, I still had a long way to go and the sun was sinking toward the horizon. So, I pressed on.

Soon after returning to the paved roads, the pain in my right shin returned with a vengeance. Despite the terrible pain, I had a certain level of comfort knowing that I was back in civilization (well, sort of). As I alluded to before, this area isn't exactly a thriving metropolis.

Yet, there were vehicles driving up and down the road and even the occasional police car should I need help.

When I called it quits for the day, the sun was long since down and the temperature was dropping. As I stood on the side of the narrow country road, I tried my best to explain to Lois where I was. Yet, without any specific landmarks to reference, we had trouble coordinating the pickup. I knew I was on the corner of Route 102 (Raymond Road) and Fremont Road, and thought I was within the town limits of Chester. The problem was, the neighboring towns of Raymond and Fremont as well as a nearby road named Chester, caused all kinds of confusion. For about 15 minutes, Lois and I reenacted the Abbott & Costello skit *Who's on First?* as we tried to figure out where the heck I was. In the end, one of the bicycle lights I used on my cross-country bike ride (and decided to bring with me ... just in case) saved the day. As Lois combed the countryside looking for me, she spotted me shivering in the dark on the side of the road with my "red blinky light" in hand.

Day 18 (9/25/14): Chester, NH to Hudson, NH [17.8 miles]

After breakfast, I went through my "pre-run" checklist as I've done each day of the run. Yep, I'm one of those crazy fools who has a checklist for everything. This list includes such things as: fill my hydration pack with water, stock it with energy bars and GUs, pack my phone charger and mace, and apply anti-chafe balm to the nether regions (we can't have chafing). Other noteworthy things on the list are: check my route and the weather forecast, put on my Road iD bracelet, and roll out my stiff legs (if I didn't do that, I'd be like the Tin Man without his oil can).

I was then driven to the now infamous corner of Route 102 (Raymond Road) and Fremont Road in Chester by Anna O'Herren. Anna is the aunt of 9-time NFL Pro Bowler and Super Bowl XL Champion, Alan Faneca. Alan and his wife Julie are the parents of Anabelle, who has Sturge-Weber syndrome, and are big-time players in the fight against the disorder. They've also been supporting our efforts for years. It seems they've now enlisted their aunt Anna and her husband Bill, who will be hosting me the next few days.

Before Anna saw me off (rather, dropped me off on the side of the road in the middle of nowhere), we agreed on a location where she'd pick me up after my run. My plan was to cover just shy of 18 miles and end my day at Walgreens in Hudson. It was a good landmark for Anna since she works for Walgreens, and for me since the store is located on Route 102 along my route.

After Anna drove away, I began warming up and noticed that my right shin wasn't having it today. Things were getting worse.... Either that or my tolerance for pain was waning. Regardless, I was determined to get my miles in and started down the narrow country road at a careful yet steady pace.

Dealing with this shin pain for over a week now, I realize this run isn't as much about physical stamina as it is about perseverance. I can't wish my shin splints away, but I can continue to treat the injury and manage the pain. I can also lessen the stress on my shin by maintaining proper form, reducing my speed, and altering my foot-strike on occasion. Of course, it's more than that. I need to be smart as well. Thus, I wore my Hokas again today, and might be wearing them for the foreseeable future. Bottom line, I need to do everything I can to get out there each day and keep moving forward.

With all this in mind, I was extra cautious during the early part of the day. And man, did I ever need to be. Route 102 twisted and turned through dense woodland (in some areas) and marshland (in others). My running (er ... limping) space was limited and my visibility around the bends was nonexistent. Navigating those windy stretches of road proved extremely stressful. And moving at a snail's pace proved mind-numbingly painful.

Running The Coast For A Cure

Eventually, I determined if I'm going to have to deal with stress and pain, I might as well shorten the length of time I have to deal with them. With that, the run/jog/limp began.

Normally, I listen to upbeat music while I run to keep my energy up. Yet, as I mentioned before, I've been using iTunes' shuffle feature to keep things fresh. Well, I might need to rethink that approach, especially when songs like Coldplay's *What If* start playing. As I listened to the lines, "Every step that you take could be your biggest mistake. It could bend or it could break. That's the risk that you take," I couldn't help but wonder if my right leg was going to break ... or if I'd already suffered a stress fracture.

As I closed in on the pickup point, a cyclist stopped to check on me. No doubt, he had seen me laboring in pain. I assured him I was alright, hoping to convince myself as much as him. It seemed to work on both accounts, at least well enough to get me to Hudson.

Not long after, I reached the Walgreens and met up with Anna and Bill. They greeted me with big smiles and a bag filled with water bottles, Honey Crisp apples, and an ice pack. Their concern for my well-being and enthusiasm for what I was doing was undeniable. As we drove to their home, I thought how fortunate I was that these kindhearted and supportive people, who like me are relatives of a little girl with Sturge-Weber syndrome, have come into my world at a time I truly needed them.

Day 19 (9/26/14): Awareness Speech at the Founders Academy

A couple of days back, Lois (the sweet lady who drove me to Lee and found me after my run on that dark and lonely country road), asked if I'd be interested in speaking at The Founders Academy, a new Charter School in Manchester where her daughter is a student. It had been almost a year since I'd given a speech, but I figured if the school wanted me to speak to their students then I wasn't going to pass up the opportunity to raise awareness about Sturge-Weber syndrome. Plus, my shin (and the rest of me) could use a rest day.

When I arrived, the school's founder, Thomas Frischknecht, greeted me and introduced me to the faculty. He then ushered me into the assembly room, where about 120 students (comprised of 6th and 7th graders) waited. After roll call, we recited the *Pledge of Allegiance,* then sang *America The Beautiful*. It was a good thing they had the words posted on the wall or I'd have been humming the tune rather than singing it.

I began my speech by telling the students about Jenna and her struggles with Sturge-Weber syndrome. Raising awareness is extremely important because it helps people recognize the symptoms, tears down the stigma of the disorder, and engenders acceptance of

Al DeCesaris

those living with it. Awareness also fosters and advances medical research and treatment.

Next, I explained the different ways I've been raising awareness and funds, specifically talking about my bike ride and run. And no talk to a group of children is complete without a tale or two about the wild animals I've encountered along the way. Snakes and spiders seem to be kid-favorites, though definitely not mine.

My talk then shifted to how we all have the power to help those in need, and how rewarding helping others can be. To help them understand, I told them how helping those in need is like giving a friend or family member a present you know they'll love; it's that feeling you get when you see their eyes light up with excitement as they open your present. As hard as the run has been, putting in the miles for Jenna and knowing how much it means to her is rewarding beyond measure.

After my talk, I took questions and was asked what my next adventure will be. *My next adventure?* The very thought of it made me chuckle. At the rate I'm going, I'll be lucky if I make it out of New Hampshire.

Two boys then offered me two crumbled dollar bills telling me they wanted the money to go toward a souvenir for Jenna. It was a touching gesture, the kind of altruistic act I pray Jenna's story inspires. I accepted the gift on her behalf and vowed to deliver those same two crumbled dollar bills to her.

That afternoon I went to the Walgreens where I ended my run yesterday to see if there were any products that could help alleviate my shin pain. After

76

Running The Coast For A Cure

explaining the nature of my injury, pharmacist Sally recommended several products and took the time to answer my questions. She then wished me good luck. I guess my limp made it apparent I needed it.

Later in the day, I spoke to one of Helene Neville's friends, Anthony Carracino, a certified fitness trainer and neuro-therapist. Anthony gave me tips on ways to address the shin pain, including taping my right ankle and doing ankle flexion exercises. He also told me that when I come through New Jersey he will do his best to help me. I hope his advice relieves the pain, but if it doesn't, I will definitely visit his facility for treatment.

That evening, Anna and Bill took me to their favorite restaurant in Nashua. It was great to spend a relaxing evening with them. And it didn't hurt that I was treated to one of the best meals I've had since the run began.

After dinner, Anna's co-worker and friend Damien came by their house with his superstar wife Colleen. She runs ultra-marathons and has even completed 100-mile races. (Yep, you read that right – 100!) I'd imagine my paltry 18 to 20-mile runs are just a warm-up for her. Colleen had all kinds of useful running tips and advice, which included putting anti-chafe balm on my toes and wearing toed socks to prevent blisters.

When I called it a night, I went to bed hopeful that all the new things I'd learned from Colleen, Anthony, and pharmacist Sally would help me manage the shin splints and blisters … and, who knows, maybe even get me back to a type of running that's a little less torturous.

77

Day 20 (9/27/14): Hudson, NH to Ayer, MA [20.1 miles]

After going through my pre-run checklist and working in all the things I learned yesterday, I enjoyed a leisurely breakfast with Anna and Bill's son Matthew (unfortunately, their other son Christopher wasn't able to join us). As we ate, we compared notes on our favorite comic book superheroes, discussed the epic fantasy tale *The Lord of the Rings* and even debated what's better: *Star Wars* or *Star Trek*. Between the two of us there's enough "*Comic-Con* knowledge" to fill the *Millennium Falcon* or the USS *Enterprise* (depending on which science fiction movie franchise you fancy).

I then drove to the Walgreens in Hudson where I last left off. The plan was to leave my car there and run roughly 20 miles to Ayer in "The Bay State," also known as "The Old Colony State" and "The Codfish State." Clearly, Massachusetts has no shortage of nicknames. Anna was to pick me up there and drive me back to my car. I was then to follow her back to her house. I admit, this isn't the most efficient way of getting around, but it's cheaper than cabs and safer than hitchhiking.

About a mile into my run, I crossed the Merrimack River and entered Nashua. On Main Street, I picked up the Nashua Heritage Rail Trail. It's just a short trail, but it

Al DeCesaris

allowed me to get off the busy streets of downtown Nashua for a while. As I ran along it, the U2 song *Sometimes You Can't Make It On Your Own* came on. When Bono sang the title line, I thought, *this sums it all up*. Without the support and encouragement of numerous people, many of which were complete strangers until recently, my accomplishments thus far, and what I hope to accomplish over the next couple of months, would not be possible.

Afterward, I spoke to one of my best friends from college and another member of my all-star medical team, doctoral physical therapist John Gallagher. John explained the specifics of shin splints and offered additional advice on ways to reduce the pain (by now I should be an expert on the subject). His advice reinforced my belief that a great number of kind and generous supporters are helping make this charity event viable.

As John and I were wrapping up our conversation, I must not have been paying attention and my feet came down within inches of a snake. I jumped to the side and shrieked like a frightened child. You'd think I would have handled the situation a little better. It's not like this was the first time this happened; but this particular snake looked extra mean and extra dangerous.

What had been a relatively pain-free day came to an abrupt end with my "serpent-side-step." The awkward leap (and even more awkward landing) caused terrible pain. As though I didn't have enough to deal with, I soon realized I'd missed a turn I was supposed to take. The

Running The Coast For A Cure

mistake forced me to backtrack and cost me a good 30 minutes. *How the heck did I miss the turn with all these navigation apps on my phone?* It might be time for turn-by-turn navigation, and for me to start watching where I'm going (and stepping).

Once I was again headed the right way, I turned onto the Nashua River Rail Trail, an 11-mile paved path that follows the course of the Nashua River and runs atop former railroad tracks. It starts within the city limits of Nashua and runs to the town of Ayer. Since Ayer was my destination, taking the trail meant I wouldn't have to worry about making any more turns (or, in my case, missing them). The trail was smooth, flat, and scenic, and the river showcased the fall colors like nothing I've seen thus far. Leaves of fiery red and orange reflected off the water and made for breathtaking vistas.

That afternoon, I entered Massachusetts. To my disappointment, there was no sign to mark the state line. Regardless, I'd made it to state number three, and was thrilled. Knowing that I'd crossed another state line made even the shin pain tolerable (well, somewhat).

When I reached the end of the trail, Anna was there waiting. The O'Herrens have been amazing and have made me feel like a part of their family. That couldn't have been easy for Anna as she was stuck in the close confines of a car with me after I had just run 20+ miles. Nope, I'm sure that wasn't easy at all.

Day 21 (9/28/14): Ayer, MA to West Boylston, MA [19.9 miles]

It was Bill who drove me to my starting point today. As we neared the location in Ayer where I left off yesterday, Bill said he could run with me for a while if I wanted him to. I didn't need convincing. I'd been running by myself almost every day for the past three weeks, having company sounded terrific.

Bill and I ran at a moderate pace and chatted as we did. You know what they say, if you can't carry a conversation while you're running, then you're running too fast (well, at least that's what I say). We were so engrossed in our conversation that we ended up missing a turn. It's ridiculous; this is becoming the norm for me. Fortunately, there was a nearby road that took us where we needed to go, and we didn't have to backtrack, this time.

It was great running with Bill. Having him with me helped keep me motivated; my pace was quicker and the number of breaks I took was down. It also helped keep my mind off my ailing shin. When we reached a good stopping point, at about the five-mile mark, Bill wished me well then started back toward his car.

At that point, I turned onto a narrow country road that wound through the woods under a canopy of autumn leaves. As I ran, woodpeckers drummed, and golden-brown acorns and brightly colored leaves rained down. Although Bill and I had just run through rural land, this particular stretch seemed much more remote and had a serene quality to it.... That was until some lunatic in a sports car flew by at breakneck speed and ruined the moment.

Soon after, my right shin started bothering me. (Big surprise, right?) It wasn't constant pain, it just seemed to come and go. However, when it did come, it was awful. And with the pain came extreme fatigue. Not that I shouldn't have been weary, I *had* run over 350 miles in three weeks, but this was worse than usual.

Complicating matters, as the day wore on, it got hot. I've been trying my best to avoid taking full-stop breaks during my runs, but today I just had to. As I made my way through the town of Clinton, I took a few minutes off and got myself a cold drink. No, not water. I'd sipped enough warm water from my hydration pack for one day. I'm talking about a fluorescent-colored sports drink. With the heat and fatigue working me over, I needed all the electrolytes (and artificial flavoring) I could get.

A little later in the day, I ran past the Wachusett Reservoir and again stopped for a break. Although this time, it wasn't the result of my wilting energy and the rising temperature (well, not completely). This stop was more about taking in the amazing views of the reservoir's calm blue waters and the lush unspoiled woodland beyond it. Despite the difficulties of the day (or maybe in spite of them), I delighted in the beauty

Running The Coast For A Cure

around me and enjoyed a few peaceful moments before the final push.

My pickup point, a salon in West Boylston, lay just on the far side of the reservoir. However, the approach took me down a series of steep, curving downward slopes. As I've said before, my shin pain isn't so bad when I'm running uphill but running downhill brings terrible pain. Over the course of those last few miles the pain got so intense it felt like my shin was going to snap and tear through the skin. Was that possible? Could the bone actually come through the skin? (From what my medical team tells me, that isn't going to happen ... though I'm not convinced.) As I slogged along, I must have looked down at my shin a half dozen times – and even stopped and ran my fingers over it – to make sure the bone was still in there and intact.

I just need to suck it up a little longer. I'm almost there, I told myself. However, I soon realized I wasn't. Every time I thought I was getting close to the pickup point, the road wound around another bend and it – and the excruciating pain – continued on and on. About that time, iTunes shuffled to the Beatles song, *The Long And Winding Road*. I thought, *how apropos.*

I'm not sure what the future holds, but as of today I can no longer run (and can barely walk) downhill. I know if I'm going to make it to Key Largo, I need to trust that my shin will hold up and resign myself to the fact that the pain might be with me the rest of the way.

Day 22 (9/29/14): West Boylston, MA to Charlton, MA [21.3 miles]

By the time I climbed out of bed, Anna, Bill, and their sons had already headed off to work and school. They did, however, leave breakfast out for me and a note letting me know that rides had been arranged for the next several days. My time with the O'Herren family has been a real blessing. Their hospitality, generosity, and support have been nothing short of amazing.

After packing my things and loading up my car, I headed to the salon in West Boylston where I left off yesterday. The plan was to leave my car there and run approximately 21 miles to an auto dealership in the town of Charlton. Anna's friend and co-worker Damien, whom I met a few nights back, would then pick me up when I finished and drive me back to my car. This, of course, was all subject to my shin's cooperation.

As I drove to West Boylston, I had the pleasure of speaking with my friend Paul Siegel. Paul is a Sturge-Weber syndrome patient I met last year while doing my cross-country bike ride. Like myself, he strives to raise awareness and funds for Sturge-Weber syndrome research and recently kicked off a campaign of his own to help the cause. Paul is also getting ready to graduate from Towson University with a degree in Mass

Communications. I love learning of his achievements and am proud to be standing with him in the search for a cure.

Once I got to the salon, I began a lengthy stretching session. Mindful of the excruciating pain I experienced at the end of yesterday's run, I wanted to make sure I was completely warmed up before I put any pressure on my shin. I also decided, if I felt like I did yesterday (even for a second), I would shut it down and walk.

Not far into the run, I came upon another slithering snake. Unlike my previous encounters, I saw this one from far enough away that I was able to maneuver around it without hurting (or embarrassing) myself. I hate seeing those scaly devils (even when they're behind glass at the zoo), but this encounter wasn't so bad. I guess I was just impressed with myself because (for once) I didn't almost step on the darn thing.

The other thing I come across a lot these days are wild grapes. For the better part of the past week, at least once a day, I've caught a whiff – and a glimpse – of the dark blue fruit hanging from vines on the side of the road. The smell of them takes me back to my youth when PB&J sandwiches were the lunch of choice. Actually, they would be now as well, if someone would make them for me.

Soon after, I reached the city of Worcester. No offense to any Bay Staters out there (I'm sure Worcester is a lovely city), but the part I ran through was anything but. The buildings were old and run-down, and the streets were covered with trash. It didn't seem like the

Running The Coast For A Cure

safest area either. Every other business was a pawn shop or a check-cashing service, and many of them had bars on the windows. I kept thinking, *it's just this one area, it'll get better soon*, but it never did. Suffice to say, no photos of Worcester are going to make the run's photo album. The quicker I forget that place the better.

As I made my way out of the city, I came upon a number of steep hills, one after the other. The ups were no fun, and the downs were downright miserable. At that point, my shin bone was still inside my leg ... and that's exactly where I wanted to keep it. So, I stopped running and began walking. My hope was that the terrain would level out, though it didn't for miles leaving me to a laborious and somewhat painful self-imposed walk.

When Damien and I talked earlier, I told him I'd reach the pickup point in Charlton between 4pm and 4:30pm. However, the hills had set me back and I didn't end up getting there until around 4:45pm. Those who know me well, know punctuality has never been my strong suit. Yet, by my standards, 15 minutes late isn't so bad. And let's be fair; I do have a good excuse for "running" late these days (bad pun intended).

Day 23 (9/30/14): Charlton, MA to Stafford Springs, CT [19.3 miles]

The day started with more assistance courtesy of Anna and Walgreens. She arranged for another of her co-workers, Paul, to pick me up at my motel and drop me off where I left off yesterday. Paul couldn't have been nicer and even offered to pick me up and bring me back to my car when I finished the day's run.

When I got started, it was cold and dreary. Although I find it difficult running when the sun is beating down on me, days like this suck the life out of me like no other. Add another snake sighting to the equation and the day was well on its way to becoming "one of those days."

As I ran down the road, I came to an area where the metal guardrail pinched in toward the roadway, leaving just a few feet between me and oncoming traffic. It was one of the most dangerous stretches of road I'd been on. At one point, two huge 18-wheelers came barreling down the road side-by-side. I pressed my body against the guardrail, closed my eyes, and hoped for the best. The trucks passed without hitting me, yet the close call made me realize how foolish I was for running on that side of the guardrail. I quickly jumped over the rail and began trudging through the bushes, tall grass, and debris on the outside of it (rather, the *right side* of it).

Al DeCesaris

Minutes later, I caught – and ripped – my shorts on the jagged metal of the back of the guardrail. They were custom-designed *Running The Coast For A Cure* shorts with the map of the East Coast on one leg and the event logo on the other. (Special thanks to Fit2Win Sportswear for the cool running shorts.) I was disappointed I'd ripped them. Though, as I watched cars and trucks whiz by absurdly close to the guardrail, I realized a torn pair of shorts was much better than the alternative.

In the afternoon, it started to drizzle. It wasn't a major problem since it was warm out and the trees provided cover. Still, I'm not keen on running in the rain. First off, slipping is a concern, especially when the ground is covered with leaves like it was today. I also worry about the visibility of drivers and the possibility of vehicles hydroplaning. Either situation could prove disastrous. I know it won't always work out (today's run is case in point), but for safety reasons I try to avoid running in the rain.

Soon after, a black cat crossed my path. *Seriously!?!* I hadn't seen a cat out on the road at any point during my run, and now I see a *black cat* and it crosses right in front of me. It had me wondering if I should just call it a day right then and there. Obviously, that wasn't going to happen, but that's definitely not the kind of thing that gives you the warm and fuzzy feeling inside.

Later, I heard something behind me and turned to see a dog scampering up beside me. He was a friendly little guy just looking to play. Although I would have loved the company, I knew his owners wouldn't be

92

Running The Coast For A Cure

happy if he came with me. So, I offered him a piece of an energy bar in hopes of convincing him to go home. He seemed about as interested in eating it as I was, though it did convince him to stop following me.

I wasn't sure when, but I knew at some point in the afternoon I would cross into Connecticut. As I ran down a windy, hilly rural road, I looked around for a sign to indicate the state line. When I didn't see anything, I wondered if I was going to enter yet another state without something to mark my achievement. However, around 2pm, I spotted a marker that read, "CONN MASS LINE." It was a terrific surprise. Not only was I able to document my run through Massachusetts, but my entry into Connecticut too, and all with one photo.

Even more exciting than locating the marker and reaching "The Constitution State," I didn't have any shin problems today. Not to say my shin wasn't still tender, but the pain I'd felt the past 10-12 days was almost nonexistent. I pray this is a sign the shin splints are behind me.

That evening I spoke to Bob Stanger, one of my childhood best friends and a huge supporter of our efforts. As he often does, Bob called to see how I was doing. Mentally I feel good, I told him. I look forward to getting out there each day to do my part for the cause. Physically though, it has been extremely difficult. The good news is, my shin is feeling much better. Bob was happy to hear that … or maybe not. He knows when I come through Virginia, I expect him to run with me; and I'm not taking no for an answer.

named Main Street) lined with shops and cafés, a small stone bridge over a lazy river, and train tracks tracing the water's winding course. On the far end of town was a dam with water trickling over the top. Around it stood trees with leaves of muted greens and others with brilliant autumn colors.

After I left town and returned to rural, tree-lined roads, it started to rain hard. And when I say hard, I'm talking the "cats and dogs" proportion. As I broke out my poncho, which I brought for such an occasion, I wondered how the weather forecasters could have been so wrong.

Proper rain gear is both functional and breathable. However, my $10 hobo poncho wasn't either. Even though it was chilly, I was sweating my tail off under that thing. Aside from that, I couldn't see peripherally because of the poncho's hood. I was also having a tough time keeping my phone dry. It seemed every time I unbuttoned (then re-buttoned) the poncho when I took out (then put away) my phone, I would have to retrieve it again to re-check my location on Google Maps. Worst of all, the poncho just extended to my knees, so my shoes and socks got soaked. Although it can be fun to go on a short run in the rain when the weather is warm, running 18+ miles in the pouring rain on unfamiliar roads with gear on your back is trying, to say the least.

The waterlogged run ended at my car. As had been arranged, Christina Lob and Andre Khatchaturian, reporters with New England Sports Network (NESN), met me there to interview me. The interview went well,

Running The Coast For A Cure

and the reporters couldn't have been nicer. Still, they did have me run an extra mile for the newscast. I guess they didn't think 18.7 miles was enough for one day.

After the interview, I drove to Dave Cooper's house in Simsbury where I'm staying for the night. Dave is yet another co-worker and friend of Anna. By the time I navigated rush hour traffic and reached his house, I was wet, cold, and tired (and a little cranky too). Yet, a warm reception from Dave, his wife Jen, their kids Kaitlyn and Josh, and their dog Cooper (which would make him, Cooper Cooper), followed by a hot shower cured all that. Dave then took me, Kaitlyn, and Josh to Plan B Burger Bar for an ice-cold beer and a mouth-watering burger.

As I settled in for the night, I couldn't help but think how fortunate I've been with my health as of late. The pain and discomfort in my right shin, which just days ago was nearly unbearable, is now barely noticeable. I can't explain it, especially in light of the fact that most everyone I talked to about it said you can't recover from shin splints unless you stop running and give your body time to heal. Even more surprising, my medical team was concerned I might have been developing a stress fracture, which could have forced me to stop running altogether. Keep in mind, I did receive advice from them and many others on various ways to treat the injury, and by and large implemented it all. I also had a great number of people praying for me. To whatever – or whomever – I owe thanks, I am eternally grateful.

Day 25 (10/2/14): Manchester, CT to Berlin, CT [18.9 miles]

After a peaceful night's sleep, I headed downstairs for breakfast. The kids had already left for school, but Dave and Jen were still home. As I ate, Dave and I chatted and shared some laughs. From the moment I arrived, Dave and his family made me feel at home. I now realize when Dave said, "my house is your house," he meant it. Spending time with the Coopers was an unexpected treat on this wild ride that has me racing headlong from one random, unfamiliar place to the next.

After saying our goodbyes, I drove to the location in Manchester where I left off. Soon after, reporter AJ Walker of WTNH News 8 arrived to interview me. (BTW it was just coincidence that the two interviews took place at the same location, on consecutive days.) It was yet another opportunity to share our message with a TV audience. Like the NESN reporters had done, AJ had me run for the camera, though this time I was able to run in the direction I needed to go. After the interview, I set out on Tolland Turnpike toward my destination of Berlin, covering the first of many miles while AJ filmed me.

Not far into it, I came to a railroad crossing just as the signal lights began to flash and the arms of the gate started to lower. Without a thought, I slipped between

Al DeCesaris

the arms of the gate and readied my iPhone for a picture. I'm not sure why, but I've always had a fascination with trains. I suppose they remind me of that old Lionel train set my family had when I was young. Every year during the holidays my siblings and I would help my parents set it up amid a miniature winter village my Mom made. Lights shone from little houses and buildings, pine trees glistened with snow covered branches, and figurines ice skated on a frozen pond. The funny thing is, that old train set probably moved faster than this one. It seemed like I had to wait an eternity for the darn thing to come into view, but when it did, I got a great picture of the red, white, and blue locomotive and its engineer.

An hour or so later, I reached Hartford, the capital of the state and the self-proclaimed "Insurance Capital of the World." As I crossed the Connecticut River, I was afforded a fantastic view of the Hartford skyline. Established close to 400 years ago, Hartford is one of the oldest cities in the United States, and for a number of years after the Civil War, one of the country's wealthiest. It was also home for a time to "The Father of American Literature" Samuel Langhorne Clemens, better known as Mark Twain.

Soon after, a woman drove by and gave me a big thumbs-up. I love encouragement like that, especially when it's unexpected. On a day like today that was cloudy and gloomy, "Thumbs-up Lady" (as she will forever be known) made it a little brighter. Another thing that made the day brighter was that my right shin felt

Running The Coast For A Cure

100%. For the first time in a long time, I was running unhindered ... and it felt incredible. I still can't explain what led to the recovery, but I thank the good Lord for it.

In the early evening, I reached my destination in Berlin and met Ron, my volunteer driver for the day. Ron was recruited by our mutual friend Elizabeth Medlock. I soon learned that Ron's youngest son was diagnosed with Epilepsy at the age of four. In hopes of helping his son and others living with Epilepsy, Ron created the *Purple Pumpkin Project* to promote awareness of the disorder. On Halloween, paint a pumpkin purple (the official color of Epilepsy) and when people ask why your pumpkin is purple, tell them about Epilepsy. It's a fun and inventive campaign, and over the past few years has really taken off.

It's kind of like what I'm doing with this charity run. When people hear about it or see me running down the road with the *Running The Coast For A Cure* logo on my apparel, it prompts them to ask what the run is all about. This creates a great opportunity to tell them about Sturge-Weber syndrome. Coincidentally, seizures are one of the many complications associated with Sturge-Weber syndrome. This I know too well because Jenna has suffered countless seizures over the years, many of which have had devastating effects.

Although I'll be on the road this Halloween, I'll see to it that Ida and Jenna paint a pumpkin purple in honor of Ron's son and help raise awareness about Epilepsy.

Day 28 (10/5/14): North Haven, CT to Stratford, CT [20.8 miles]

Yesterday morning I woke to heavy rain and decided to take the day off. It was a good decision because it ended up pouring almost the entire day. I spent my "rain day" in the warm, dry confines of Laurie's cottage. More accurately, I spent it in bed. There are few people who like their sleep as much as I do.

When the rain finally let up, I went out for dinner. After eating energy and protein bars for both breakfast and lunch, I needed something that didn't have a 10-year shelf life and the word "bar" in it. Laurie had recommended The Red Tomato Pizzeria (in the neighboring town of Madison) for New Haven-style pizza. I wasn't sure what New Haven-style meant, but I was in the mood for pizza (I pretty much always am).

They say what differentiates New Haven-style (locally known as "apizza") from all the rest, is its chewy texture, lack of mozzarella, and thin, oblong crust, which is baked and charred in a coal-fire oven. I'm no culinary expert, but over the years I've had all kinds of pizza and I will say, New Haven-style "apizza" is among the best.

As I headed out with a full and happy belly, I bumped into Heather, one of the pizzeria's owners. Heather saw my *Running The Coast For A Cure* car magnets (yep, I have magnets on my car. I'm trying to raise awareness any and every way I can) and was interested in learning about Sturge-Weber syndrome. She even offered to put information about my run in the pizzeria to help spread the word. It's supportive folks like Heather who are making our efforts a success.

This morning I woke to beautiful weather and left-over "apizza" (even cold it was delicious). After eating, I suited up, packed my things, and took in the amazing view from Laurie's cottage one last time. Unlike yesterday, when visibility was pretty much non-existent, today the sun glistened off the tranquil blue waters of the Long Island Sound with promise. As far as water views go, this one is tough to beat.

I then drove back to Bell Nurseries where I left off the day before last. I parked in their lot and went inside to get permission to leave my car there for the day. I don't often do this, but now that I'm getting into more populated areas, it's something I know I should do. The last thing I need is my car getting towed.

After getting the thumbs-up from the employees, I surveyed the road, trying to figure out which way I was supposed to go. For the life of me, I couldn't remember from which direction I'd come. I then looked at the position of the sun to try to get my bearings. However, that just left me more confused. In the end, the compass application on my phone helped me sort it out and got me going in the right direction. When people say, "I'm lost without my phone," they don't know the half of it.

Al DeCesaris

they'd brought ice, food, and drinks. After a long day on the road, that sort of thing goes a long way with me.

As we drove back to North Haven, we chatted about my run and their upcoming nuptials. They were so excited about what I'm doing and couldn't have been more supportive. Although our time together was brief, it was nice to reconnect with an old friend and make a new one in Craig. And it was good to know that I'd see them again the day after next since they had offered to give me a ride that day too.

After Lizzy and Craig dropped me off at my car, I drove back to the motel in Stratford where they had picked me up and where I happen to be staying for the night. Every now and then our "driverless-system" is surprisingly efficient and makes my days of nervous hitchhiking seem hard to believe they ever took place.

When I started this charity run, I didn't have a clue how I was going to get around. Without a dedicated driver, I wondered if the logistics could even work. Yet, almost every single day kind, caring, and generous individuals have gone out of their way to help me. For me, this has been both amazing and inspiring. Still, I'm not ready to let my unnamed old friend (you know, the one who cancelled on me) off the hook. She still has some groveling to do.

Running The Coast For A Cure

The first few hours of the run weren't very exciting, but in the early afternoon I reached New Haven. As luck would have it, Google Maps' walking route took me past the Peabody Museum of Natural History, Yale University, New Haven Green (a traditional town green that hosts public events, concerts, and park activities), and other notable landmarks. Founded by the English Puritans in the 1630's, New Haven is an old yet modern city with character and charm.

As I ran out of the city, I turned onto Route 1, the familiar highway (well, at least it is to me). Route 1 is the longest north-south highway in the United States and runs some 2,300 miles from the top of Maine to the bottom of Florida. This stretch was much busier than most of what I'd run on in Maine. It has two lanes going in each direction with lots of businesses along the roadway. Getting into a rhythm was difficult because every few minutes I had to stop at an intersection or wait as cars pulled in and out of parking lots.

Despite the chaotic nature of the road, I felt great physically and covered ground much quicker than I normally do. In fact, I made such good time I had to slow down a bit. Otherwise, I would have reached my destination in Stratford well before my ride and would have just ended up having to wait.

When I reached the pickup point, I was greeted by family friend Lizzy Duffy, her fiancé Craig, and their dog Malcolm. I hadn't seen Lizzy in years. It was really great to see her again and meet Craig. It was also great that

Day 29 (10/6/14): Stratford, CT to Darien, CT [19.4 miles]

Since I finished yesterday's run at my motel, there was no need to drive somewhere today to get started. And since my ride couldn't pick me up until 5pm, there was no reason to hit the road early. Relaxing mornings like this don't come often, so I took the opportunity to catch up on my sleep (as though I didn't get enough during the recent rain day).

After eating and going through my morning routine, I set out for what was to be a 19.4-mile run to the town of Darien. Not but a few blocks from the motel, I came to a neglected and seemingly unsafe neighborhood. I raced through it with a watchful eye (hopeful that if anyone wanted to do me harm, they weren't in the mood to chase after me).

I soon found myself in an industrial section of Bridgeport. It's the most populated city in Connecticut, and at the present has a lot of road construction going on (at least the part I was in did). As I ran through a construction site, one of the workers said, "that's a good pace. I could keep up with you." I imagine he could. I tend to maintain a slow, safe pace (when I'm not running through suspect neighborhoods, that is). I invited him to join me, but I don't think his boss was keen on him going for a run while he was on the clock.

I then went through a rundown part of Bridgeport that made the neighborhood near the motel seem like Beverly Hills. Quite a few police cars patrolled the area. Were they there because something had happened? … because something was about to happen? Who knows, maybe they were there for my protection.

Whatever the case, with several police cruisers around, I felt more or less safe. Still, I did run at a quicker pace than I normally do and made good time. Like yesterday, I had to make sure not to run too fast because it would be pointless to reach the pickup point before my ride did.

When I got to the neighborhood of Black Rock, the surroundings improved considerably. It's a vibrant part of the city with lots of cool cafes, restaurants, shops, and art galleries. Along that stretch of Route 1, Bridgeport gave way to the town of Fairfield.

As I ran through downtown Fairfield, I spotted a sculpture of Mark Twain sitting on a park bench outside of a candy store. I couldn't help but grab the seat next to him. To commemorate my visit with "The Father of American Literature," I snapped a selfie as we posed for the camera … well, one of us did.

Farther down the road, I came to Westpoint, an upscale area with high-end shops. I then crossed the Saugatuck River by way of the "Star-Spangled Bridge." (It's not actually called that. Its boring, uninspiring name is the Saugatuck River Bridge.) Along its entire length,

Running The Coast For A Cure

the red, white, and blue stars and stripes of the American Flag waved in the breeze. It's super patriotic and deserving of a proud patriotic name. So, for what it's worth, I'm giving it one.

As I neared my destination in Darien, my right heel started to hurt. I wasn't sure what had triggered the pain. For certain, the Newton Gravity III's I was wearing had serious mileage on them and probably needed to be replaced. Whether the pain was the result of overuse of my right foot or overuse of my right shoe, I decided to retire the Newtons after today's run. Obviously, retiring my foot wasn't an option.

As I jogged the last few hundred yards to my pickup point, I saw a man standing on the sidewalk urging me on. Although I'd never met him, I figured he must be Joseph, the friend of my cousin Dominick Schina, who had agreed to give me a ride. Joseph's enthusiasm, though flattering, had me chuckling. How could it not? I was jogging down the sidewalk outside of a Bertucci's restaurant while some random guy clapped and cheered with enthusiasm just as the early-bird dinner crowd (you know, the blue-hairs) were arriving.

While Joseph drove me back to Stratford, I learned that he's a lawyer like myself. After talking shop, he told me that he would be in South Florida in December and could help me with rides. It was a kind offer, though with friends living down that way, it's one of the few areas I should have my rides covered. Now, should Joseph be in Key Largo when I finish the run, we could definitely catch up for some "Sunshine State" celebrating.

Day 30 (10/7/14): Darien, CT to Mamaroneck, NY [19.9 miles]

In the morning, I drove back to Bertucci's in Darien. After parking my car in their lot, I entered the day's ending address into Google Maps, stretched out my legs, strapped on my hydration pack, and began what was to be my last day in Connecticut.

Since I had problems with my heel yesterday, I decided to walk for a while to really loosen up the muscles and tendons in my foot. As I walked, I talked on the phone with my younger brother Michael. He was instrumental in helping make my bike ride a success and is working on a number of things to help with the run. I may be on the road alone, but my family is doing a tremendous amount of work behind the scenes. I liken it to the famous saying: "Team work divides the task and multiplies the success." Now, if only I could get my little bro to run some of these miles.

After I got off the phone, I started jogging and was happy to find that my heel felt okay. I guess yesterday's pain *was* the result of worn out shoes. Still, I knew I needed to be careful with it and diligent about minimizing risks. Just because I retired those shoes and was feeling better today doesn't mean what happened yesterday didn't happen … or couldn't happen again.

Al DeCesaris

Not long after, I stepped between two buildings to take a bathroom break. Oh, come now. Don't shake your head in disapproval. When you're running 5+ hours a day, sometimes you have to go when there aren't facilities around. In congested areas such as this, going behind a dumpster or between buildings seems to work just fine. However, on this occasion, a shopkeeper came around the corner to see what I was doing. Fortunately, I saw the woman before I started and pretended like I was just looking at my cell phone. I then continued down the road as though nothing was awry. It was a close call that would have left me utterly embarrassed for urinating in public and heavily fined for public urination. Even though I managed to escape the situation with my integrity and wallet intact, it had me thinking that I might need to ease up on my coffee-intake in the mornings.

Later in the day, I had a scare of another kind. Google Maps' turn-by-turn navigation (which, since I've been using it, has worked fairly well), told me to take a left onto US 1 North. *North?!? Why on earth would I need to go north?* I almost had heart failure thinking that I'd somehow inverted my starting and ending points and was heading back to Darien. I'll admit, I've made some directional missteps, but even I couldn't make a mistake of that magnitude. Could I? Lucky for me, I hadn't. Google Maps just mentioned north because the road split and it wanted me to follow the north bound lanes, not actually go north.

A few minutes later, I caught sight of a sign that read, "WELCOME TO NEW YORK The Empire State," and

Running The Coast For A Cure

was filled with an incredible sense of accomplishment. Reaching New York meant I had just completed my run through New England (which after everything I've encountered is kind of unbelievable) and was now beginning the next stage of the journey. It was fitting too because today was the 30th day of the run; one month down and one major hurdle (New England) behind me.

After snapping my requisite state-sign-selfie, I texted the picture to my family and friends to share the news (I think I must have sent it to half of my address book). Eventually, I had to stop with the texts. If I'd lingered any longer, I wouldn't have made it to the pickup point on time. It was worth it though because I received the most encouraging responses (and some funny ones too) making the last few miles a piece of cake.

With a spring in step, I reached the pickup point, the Mamaroneck Motel (where I'm staying for the night) right on time. Well, not *right* on time, but about as on time as I can be when traveling on foot. There, I met Lizzy and was welcomed with a big smile and big bag of ice. As I iced my legs, she drove us to pick up Craig. They then took me to one of their favorite restaurants in their hometown of Stamford, Connecticut, where we had an outstanding meal and a fantastic time.

After dinner, Lizzy and Craig dropped me off at my car in Darien and we said our goodbyes. I'd be remiss if I didn't mention how wonderful it was to reconnect with them and how much I appreciate their kindness. I then drove back to New York where the next leg of this grueling, yet gratifying journey is just beginning.

Day 31 (10/8/14): Mamaroneck, NY to Moonachie, NJ [21 miles]

When I woke up this morning and got a good look at my motel room, I wondered if I should have slept atop the covers rather than under them. I must have been wearing rose-colored glasses last night because this place was disgusting. It did have some redeeming qualities however; for one it was located right on my route and … it was located right on my route. Okay, so maybe it had only one redeeming quality.

I booked out of there (I was eager to put some distance between myself and that petri dish of a motel) and headed to the day's ending point in Moonachie only to sit in bumper-to-bumper traffic. Getting through New York, across the Hudson River, and into New Jersey took forever. It didn't help that I didn't know where I was going. I was used to straightforward drives, but this one was chock full of congestion and confusion, requiring serious effort and patience. Eventually, I managed to get there, but it wasn't without wrong turns and road rage.

At the ending point, Segovia Restaurant, I met Russ, a friend of Helene Neville, who offered to help. I hopped in his car and he navigated those same congested, confusing roads (minus the wrong turns and road rage) and got me to Mamaroneck in half the time it took me.

Al DeCesaris

When I started my run, I headed southwest down Route 1 through Westchester County toward New York City. It was an easy and peaceful run early on. But, the farther I went the more crowded it got. And when I reached New York City, the Bronx to be exact, it got packed and hectic, and a bit seedy as well.

As I ran through New York City's northernmost borough, I got a lot of strange looks. And these weren't the curious stares I've been known to elicit; these were the kind that made me put my guard up. With my head down (careful not to make eye contact with anyone), I weaved in and out of the crowds as quickly as I could, then raced through Bronx Park, past Fordham University, and west over the Harlem River.

Before I knew it, I was approaching the George Washington Bridge, which spans the Hudson River and links New York City and New Jersey. I've driven across the bridge a number of times, but never had I thought about running across it. Actually, until a few days ago, I didn't even know you could. As you can imagine, with an upper level of eight lanes and a lower level of six, crossing the soaring dual-towered, double-decked suspension bridge on foot is an experience unto itself. On foot you can hear the wind whipping through the cables and suspenders, feel the bounce and sway of the roadway, and see the multitude of vehicles zooming by. From the pedestrian area, I had an amazing view of the Manhattan skyline. Although I was happy to leave the chaos of New York City behind, the view of it from the bridge was a sight to behold.

Running The Coast For A Cure

I crossed the remainder of the bridge and stepped into New Jersey, my sixth state. Yet, I couldn't mark my achievement because there was no sign welcoming me. As you know, without a selfie to commemorate an occasion, it might as well not have happened.

Soon after, I ran out of steam, making the last six miles onerous. Worse yet, I ended up on a major road with heavy traffic and a narrow shoulder. It was one of those roads I just knew I shouldn't be on. *What the heck is Google Maps doing to me?* I asked with a few choice words sprinkled in. After a nervous sprint, I found a spot where I could get onto a less congested parallel road and reached the day's ending point not long after.

The stress of the situation and the disappointment of not getting my state-sign-selfie was soon forgotten when I saw my hotel. This was no dingy roadside motel that left me wondering what a black-light might reveal. This was a proper hotel with clean sheets and mini soaps and mini shampoos (clearly, it doesn't take much to impress me these days). The room was compliments of Will Futch, one of my best friends from High School. Just as he had during my bike ride, he offered to book a few rooms for me in support of the cause.

Yesterday's run marked a significant achievement, yet reaching New Jersey was significant in its own right. The road ahead was familiar territory with several good friends living along the way. Whether justified or not, I felt I could breathe a little easier now that I'd reached the "peace and tranquility" of "The Garden State."

Day 32 (10/9/14): Moonachie, NJ to Florham Park, NJ [21.6 miles]

I woke to itchy ankles and looked down to see that my skin was red and irritated. Was it a rash from the tape I'd been putting on my ankles? Was it poison ivy? Oh, I really hoped it wasn't poison ivy. I've gotten some nasty cases of it over the years. Whether I touch it or not, it ends up spreading all over my body. And when I say all over my body, I'm talking *everywhere*. I did my best to cover it with my socks and compression sleeves.

I then headed to the day's ending point in Florham Park. According to my family, the ending point was a business right along my route with a parking lot where I could leave my car. However, that's not what I found when I got there. The address they gave me was for a house in a neighborhood off the main road. I thought that maybe they had just typed the address incorrectly when they texted it to me. But I knew that wasn't the case when I saw Russ, who was again helping me, there as well. We obviously had a bad address, and I couldn't just leave my car there.

As my team back home tried to figure things out, Russ and I waited … and waited. I soon grew annoyed (as you know, patience isn't a virtue of mine). I could only imagine what Russ was thinking. At the very least, he probably wondered how the heck I'd made it this far (truth be told, sometimes I wonder that too). After 45 minutes of internet research and a lot of back and forth on the phone, we found a new ending point. As fast as we could, Russ and I drove there, I parked my car, and Russ gave me a lift back to Moonachie. The whole annoying ordeal cost me about an hour. Not the way you want to start the day, though it would have been worse if Russ hadn't been there to help me work through it.

It wouldn't have been such a big deal if I had a full day to get my miles in, but I had a fundraising event this evening. After the day's run, I was to drive to John Gallagher's house, about an hour from my ending point. We'd then drive to his cousin Peter's restaurant to meet a group of John's friends and family who were coming out to support the cause. Also factoring in, today was to be one of the longest runs thus far (over 21 miles). So clearly, I didn't have time for that logistical nightmare.

The first seven miles of the run took me through Rutherford, Lyndhurst, and across the Passaic River into Nutley. Despite all the different areas I ran through, the sights went unnoticed. I was still irritated and just burning off my frustration. Running is good for that. Not to say it's a cure all, but it definitely helps.

Around 1pm, Google Maps led me down a shaded path through a park. It was a serene oasis with a narrow tree-lined river running the length of it. It was a nice sojourn from the cars and traffic lights and made what remained of my earlier frustrations melt away.

Running The Coast For A Cure

Later, I faced a climb that seemed to go on and on. I had no idea how high it actually went. Every time I thought I reached the top the road would bend, and the upslope would continue. Scaling it was quite a challenge, but one that I relished now that I was running without pain. When I reached the top and looked back, I had a fantastic view of the New York City skyline. I suppose that was a reward for my hard work, though the reward I enjoyed most was the downhill that followed.

I ended up finishing the run – all 21.6 miles of it – in decent time and even managed to get to John's house without getting lost. Although I talk to John often (like every other day about this injury or that), it has been some time since I last saw him. Reconnecting with my old college friend was awesome. It was also great to meet his adorable newborn son John Jr.

After catching up, we headed over to the restaurant for the event. Along with John's friends, who came out in support of the cause, were his wife Alexia, their children Kaitlyn and John Jr., and Alexia's father James and her brother Kerry. Between mouthfuls of food and sips of beer (don't judge, it was just for the carbs), I told everyone about Sturge-Weber syndrome. My hope is that with everyone I speak to I raise awareness about the disorder. However, on this night I'm not sure how well I did ... I was competing with an NFL football game on the TVs at the bar. Still, with John and Alexia's help, we raised a lot of money for Sturge-Weber syndrome research. It might not have been the smoothest of days, but it definitely was a fun and successful night.

Day 33 (10/10/14): Florham Park, NJ to Bridgewater, NJ [23.5 miles]

I began the day with breakfast and a cup of joe. My morning coffee is almost as important as my morning meal. I can't go on a five-hour run without having coffee and giving it time to work its magic. After I ate (and let the coffee take care of business), I said my goodbyes to the Gallaghers and headed out. It was great to see John and his family. Their loyal and generous support over the years has been phenomenal.

By the time I got to Florham Park and began my run, it was close to noon. You would think I'd have gotten an early start considering I had the biggest day yet ahead of me (23.5 miles) and needed to be in Bridgewater by 6pm to meet my ride. But that would have made too much sense. Evidently, I prefer to work under pressure, the more the better. Adding stress to an already stressful situation was the weather. It was chilly and the sky was overcast. *Were those rain clouds?* I hoped not.

About an hour in I saw the Grim Reaper shrouded in a black cloak standing amid tombstones. With an outstretched arm, he beckoned me. The sight of him stopped me dead in my tracks. Granted, he was an inflatable lawn decoration and the tombstones were made of plastic and said things like "They Taxed Me To

Death," but he *was* 20 feet tall and had piercing red eyes for crying out loud. I realize Halloween is right around the corner, but was the "deliverer of death" really necessary? A few pumpkins would have sufficed.

Google Maps then led me to Great Swamp National Wildlife Refuge. It appeared to be an isolated wooded area, navigable only on foot. I knew should a problem arise I'd be on my own. However, doubling back would have cost me too much time, so against my better judgment, I charged ahead. The trail soon degraded into little more than a narrow path of trampled grass meandering through dense woodland. In certain areas, it was so overgrown it was difficult to tell whether I was still even on it. Even more concerning was what could have been lurking in the "wildlife" refuge. I was wearing my compression sleeves, which protected my legs from thorns and poison ivy, but they weren't going to do any good if I got bit by a snake or some other carnivorous creature.

I was on the "trail" for about three miles, running where I could, walking where I had to, and jumping over anything that moved. I knew I had pushed my luck and was just waiting for something to sink its teeth into me. Yet, somehow, I managed to evade the reaper and made it to the other side of the refuge with nothing more than a few scrapes and some hitchhikers on my clothes.

Soon after, it started to drizzle. *Not good!* I still had a lot of miles to cover and scant time to do it. The excursion through the woods (and my laissez fare

Running The Coast For A Cure

attitude this morning) had set me back. I picked up the pace and hoped the drizzle didn't turn into a downpour.

In the late afternoon, I got an encouraging message from one of my great friends, Brian Hockin. Brian is an officer in the U.S. Navy, serving in Afghanistan. With everything going on over there for him to take the time to send me a message meant a lot to me. It also had me laughing because he asked how I was going to top this. *One thing at a time, Brian, one thing at a time.*

Lucky for me, the hard rain held off and I was able to complete this "one thing" (which just so happened to be the most miles I've ever run), right on time. At the pickup point, I met my volunteer driver and dear old friend, Stephanie Cachianes. Our fathers are childhood friends, so Stephanie and I met before I can even remember. As kids, we spent our summers together at the beach in Ocean City, Maryland, and then went to college together at the University of Delaware. Although we hadn't seen each other in years, we picked up right where we left off. What a treat it was to spend time with her.

After she dropped me off at my car, I drove to the home of yet another great friend, Brian McCabe. I had gone to grade school and high school with Brian and his wife Julie. They had been kind enough to invite me to stay with them while I ran through the area. As I've said before, this run is no easy feat. But days like today, when I'm blessed to be in the company of (and communicate with) such caring and supportive friends, make the trials and tribulations (and Grim Reapers and swamp hazards) much more manageable.

129

Day 34 (10/11/14): Bridgewater, NJ to Ringoes, NJ [19.2 miles]

I enjoyed breakfast in the company of the McCabe kids: Addie, Kathryn, and Andrew. Brian and Julie must have been keeping them abreast of my run because they seemed to know all about it; the good, the bad, and the injuries. I think Brian and Julie may have had them read my *Crossing America For A Cure* book as well because they seemed to know everything about my bike ride too. They even asked me to sign their copy of it. I must admit, when I'm asked to autograph my books, I get a little embarrassment. But How could I not sign it? The McCabes purchased one of the very first copies I sold.

As I readied to head out, Julie gave me energy bars with real coconut, cubes of frozen wheatgrass, and a Steaz organic energy drink. I wasn't sure what to make of all this healthy stuff. I was used to eating and drinking whatever prepackaged, processed, artificially flavored junk I could find at a convenience store. "Real" and "organic" weren't exactly in my vocabulary, but I figured if I was going to follow anyone's lead on eating and drinking right, it'd be Julie's. She's a neo-natal intensive care nurse and a connoisseur of all things healthy.

I followed Brian to the day's ending point, a country market in Ringoes. After making sure it was okay to leave my car in their parking lot, I hopped into Brian's car, and he drove me back to where I left off yesterday.

It was a cold and dreary day, which tends to make it difficult to loosen up and get going. The weather has always had a big effect on me. I remember when I was a kid how I struggled to get out of bed during the winter months (and on occasion still do). Give me the heat over the cold any day of the week. And sunshine ... I'm one of those people who needs plenty of it to keep my spirits up.

Although I didn't get any sunshine today, I had Brian running with me for the first few miles, which was a big help. Brian, like Bill O'Herren, is one of those rare triple-threat volunteers: host, driver, and guest runner. It was great to have the company and to share this experience with my childhood friend.

The day's route took me over brooks and past woodland, crop fields, and horse farms. I had no idea how much rural land there is in New Jersey and how scenic it is. I thought I knew the state well, but I suppose driving the Jersey Turnpike on the way to New York City doesn't exactly qualify me as a "Garden State" expert.

Unlike yesterday, today I was under no time restriction and the run was only about 19 miles. *Only 19?* Don't you love how one day your stressing about something that seems insurmountable, then the next you're making an off-hand comment about how that's all you have to do, like it's no problem whatsoever.

That's the interesting thing about this run. Each day I'm tasked with covering distances that most people think are far too great to sustain for any significant length of time. Some people train for months to run a distance like this on just one occasion. Keep in mind, I'm not pointing this out because I think I'm some amazing athlete or that I possess the strength the average person doesn't. At 5'7 (or so my driver's license says) and 150 pounds, *I am* the average person. The bottom line is I believe we *all* have the power within us to accomplish such things. This ordinary man doing what others deem extraordinary is living proof of that.

Late in the day, I developed discomfort in my left Soleus (a muscle in the back part of the lower leg, which runs from below the knee to the heel). I had experienced a Soleus injury of my right leg last March while training. What had started as subtle pain and minor swelling turned into a nagging injury that sidelined me for a couple of weeks. The last thing I needed was another problem like that.

Lucky for me, this didn't seem as bad as that, and it didn't slow me down much. In fact, I ended up finishing the day's run in good time. It must have been the positive attitude … then again it could have been the coconut bars or that oh so tasty wheat grass.

Day 35 (10/12/14): Ringoes, NJ to Warrington, PA [21.7 miles]

After breakfast, Brian and I chatted with our old high school buddy, Will Futch. Aside from hooking me up with free hotel rooms, Will always has me laughing. He's one of those guys who seems to have a never-ending cache of ridiculous stories bordering on the absurd (you know the type). Brian is pretty darn funny in his own right, and between the two of them the comedy routine had me in stitches.

When the show was over, Brian and I headed to the day's ending point in Warrington, Pennsylvania. First, we made a quick stop at a shopping center in Pennington to see Babe The Blue Star Ox. Babe is part of *Stampede*, an outdoor art exhibit hosted by the Hopewell Valley Arts Council. Julie thought it'd be great for me to get a picture in front of Babe since the ox's patriotic colors (that's code for red, white, and blue) matched my running apparel. I thought the idea was silly at first, but when I saw how well the picture turned out I was quite pleased with how Babe and I looked together.

Despite the side trip visiting the bovine babe, we reached the day's ending point, Valley Square shopping center on Route 611, in good time. I then hopped in

Al DeCesaris

Brian's car and he gave me a ride back to the country market in Ringoes where I ended my run yesterday.

Unlike the past few days, today it was sunny and beautiful; my kind of day for a run. Actually, it was my kind of day for any outdoor activity. It just so happens that these days a 20-some-odd-mile run is my only option.

My route again took me through scenic rural land. And when I say "scenic" and "rural" I'm talking farms with red gable-roofed barns and stacked stone dividing walls; idyllic country scenes of simpler times.

As I moved into a more populated area, I met a man working on his house. He was curious to know what I was doing. I was happy to share my story and raise awareness about the cause. However, getting back on the road wasn't easy. Every time I tried to leave, the man asked another question and kept talking ... and talking. It was plain to see he meant well, but it seemed there was no end in sight. I had to use every trick in the book to get out of the verbal headlock he had me in.

A mile or so farther down the road, I reached Lambertville. It's a charming little city with both 18th and 19th century architecture and a bunch of restaurants, shops, galleries, and inns. The streets were packed with people milling about, making for a lively atmosphere.

Before reaching the bridge that spans the Delaware River to New Hope, Pennsylvania, I looked over my shoulder and saw a "Welcome to New Jersey" sign. I was excited and relieved to see it since I didn't get my picture in front of a New Jersey sign when I entered the

Running The Coast For A Cure

state. After my state sign photo shoot, I continued toward the bridge, eager to reach my seventh state.

At the mid-way point of the pedestrian section of the bridge, I saw the words "New Jersey" painted on the ground and just beyond it "Pennsylvania." I snapped a couple of quick pics and thought, *that's cool but there better be a sign I can take a selfie in front of.* Reaching "The Keystone State" was one thing; but getting a picture to memorialize my achievement was what I was after. Obviously, my priorities are a little out of whack these days.

Thankfully for me (and my OCD tendencies), there was a Pennsylvania sign on the far side of the bridge. The catch was, it was on the other side of a guardrail. But you know me, I wasn't going to be denied. I hopped the guardrail and ... that's when the pandemonium broke out. A guard in the gatehouse started screaming at me as though I'd just jumped the fence at the White House. For the record, I have great respect for law enforcement, but when a glorified traffic guard starts chastising me like I'm an insolent child, I have to put my foot down. A contentious argument ensued. In the end, I got my selfie (though the top of my head was cut off) and got out of there before Mr. Friendly called the authorities.

New Hope had a similar look and feel as Lambertville. And like its neighbor to the east, it had throngs of people strolling the streets. As I ran through town (looking over my shoulder for the cops as I did), I passed a bevy of restaurants, antique shops, and art

137

galleries. There's even a well-known theater where Broadway shows are previewed. Yet, even more interesting (at least to me), just six miles north is the spot where George Washington crossed the Delaware River. What can I say? I'm a bit of a history buff.

Once I got beyond New Hope, the road became narrow, windy, and hilly. Roads like this tend to make me nervous, but this stretch was even more nerve-wracking because a number of drivers seemed angry that I was there. They must have been related to that lunatic traffic guard. One even went so far as to give me the one finger salute. And no, it wasn't to tell me I was number one.

After I finished my run, I drove back to New Hope to get a better picture in front of the Pennsylvania sign (one where my head wasn't cut off). This time there was a guard named Linda on duty. After I told her what I was doing, she let me get behind the guardrail and even offered to take the picture for me. Her kindness, and the other guard's hostility, reminded me just how important proper communication is. He probably thought I was some delinquent trying to stir up trouble whereas she knew what I was doing and why I wanted the picture. That doesn't explain away the road rage directed at me, but it might let Mr. Friendly off the hook.

Day 36 (10/13/14): Warrington, PA to Villanova, PA [21.8 miles]

Once today's run was completed, I would be too far from the McCabe's house to come all the way back; it was time to move on. After saying goodbye to Brian, Julie, and their kids and thanking them for their hospitality (and the wheat grass … it had started to grow on me), I drove back to the shopping center in Warrington where I left off.

The plan was to leave my car there, run about 22 miles to the outskirts of Villanova, then get a ride back to my car from my cousin Dominick Schina. After that, I'd drive to the home of Laurie Rostock's parents in Media where I'm staying for the night. It was a lot of driving and a lot of running. Yet, on days like this, it's working out the logistics that seems to be the most daunting task.

Not far into the run, I came to a shoulder-less stretch of road that wound through the woods. This happens on occasion (you've heard me complain about it enough to know), but when it does there's usually an area to the side of the road that I can move into should I need to avoid oncoming traffic. But, not here. I had to straddle the white line and pray the drivers saw me.

Still, the terrain was pretty. I ran past creeks, streams, and canals. Another thing that caught my

Al DeCesaris

attention was how much green there was in the leaves. Not to say they hadn't started to turn (it *was* mid-October), but they weren't as far along in the process as I'd seen.

Just after 1pm, I saw two horses grazing in a field. They were a good distance from me, but there was no mistaking what I saw in the one: unpigmented skin and a coat of white hair. It was a true white horse; a rare sight and a thing of beauty.

A little while after, I reached Ambler. It's a cute town (or, as they say in Pennsylvania, "borough") with a main drag with restaurants, shops, and a famous Spanish Colonial style theater called the Ambler Theater. It was opened by Warner Bros. in 1928 and restored not too long ago to its former glory by a nonprofit community organization that now owns it.

Minutes later, it started drizzling. And in short order a thick fog settled in over the town. It was eerie, but also rather cool. It ended up drizzling on and off for the next few hours, though (to my delight) no heavy rains fell as I made my way through Conshohocken and over the Schuylkil River.

The last couple of miles had me on a narrow, windy road with no shoulder. Sound familiar? I think this is the norm in these parts. Complicating matters, my left Soleus started to hurt again. Yet, I soon forgot the pain when a car barreled by at breakneck speed, just inches from me. Nope, Soleus wasn't bothering me at all anymore.

Running The Coast For A Cure

Despite the ominous fog, ailing Soleus, and maniac driver, I reached the address I'd been given in decent time (that is if you call five hours decent time). However, the rural setting had me wondering whether I was in the right place. This wasn't the outskirts of Villanova as I'd been told ... this was the sticks. *This can't be right.* After a phone call to my family (and a lengthy debate), I learned that I *was* in the right spot. Apparently, a random farmhouse in the middle of nowhere was the best landmark they could find.

I met up with Dominick soon after. It had been a long time since we'd seen each other, so there was a lot of catching up to do. We swapped stories over a couple of Philly cheesesteaks. When in Rome, right? He then drove me around an area of suburban Philadelphia, known as the Main Line, to show me his old stomping grounds. After Dom's Philly 'burbs tour, he drove me back to Warrington to my car. Spending the evening with cousin Dom was a real treat ... as was the cheesesteak.

I then headed to the home of Laurie's parents, Catherine and Franklin Koch, in Media. The drive there was a complete debacle. I drove for almost 45 minutes before realizing I was going the wrong way. Then, after driving that same distance back, I exited onto the wrong highway and went another 15 minutes in the wrong direction. At that point there was steam coming out of my ears. Adding insult to injury, I drove past a half dozen hotels along the way. I was exhausted and angry, and wanted nothing more than to check into one and

Al DeCesaris

call it a night, but Ida told me I'd better not. The Kochs had prepared their guest room and were waiting for me to get there. Now, I love my sister, but if she were in the car with me I think I would have strangled her. I must give her credit though because she handled my toddler temper tantrum like a champ. And during it all, she was also nice enough to navigate me in the right direction.

It was well past 10pm when I reached Media, and I was starving. I spotted a Chick-fil-A not far from the Koch's house and thought it best to get some food in my belly before calling it a night (as though a cheesesteak wasn't enough). I wolfed down a chicken sandwich and waffle fries like it was my job.

When I got to the Koch's house, I was greeted with open arms and made to feel right at home. There was just one problem, Catherine had made dinner for me. I didn't have the heart to tell her I had already eaten ... *twice*. So, after a cheesesteak and a chicken sandwich and fries, I ate a full blown three-course meal. The food was delicious but getting it down was a challenge. Just when I thought we were finished, Catherine and Franklin started in on how I needed to have seconds and weren't taking no for an answer. After all that, it was time for dessert... When dinner was finally done, I was *done* .... physically, mentally, and stomach-achingly.

Day 37 (10/14/14): Villanova, PA to Wilmington, DE [21.4 miles]

When you're doing some crazy adventure like this by yourself it means a lot when people open their homes to you. Since I've been on the road, I've had the good fortune of having friends old and new host me. I think the best part of it (aside from the free food) is getting to spend time with my hosts.

During breakfast, which this time was just one meal (thank goodness!), I learned that Franklin is a decorated World War II veteran, who served in the Navy as a Seabee (Naval Construction Forces) in the Pacific theater. His story was remarkable and had me marveling at the sacrifices he and his brothers-in-arms made for our country. What an honor it was to spend time with a real American hero.

Afterward, I packed my things, loaded up my car, and readied to leave. The plan was for me to drive my car to the day's ending point in Wilmington, Delaware, leave it there, and the Kochs would drive me back to the location where I left off yesterday. Even though the Kochs lived in the area, I decided to lead the way (why? I haven't a clue). I entered the address in my car's navigation system and started off with the Kochs following in their car.

Al DeCesaris

If you thought last night's drive went badly, you haven't heard anything yet. Because of heavy traffic, it took forever to get to Wilmington. Then, about two miles from our destination we came upon an area undergoing all kinds of road construction that had me totally confused. I wasn't sure which way to go, but for some reason I decided to get into the far right lane, which had me headed toward an onramp onto a major highway. Realizing that I wasn't supposed to get on the highway, at the last second, I swerved into the lane to the left of me and continued going straight.

Franklin and Catherine, who were a few cars behind, must not have seen what I did and were still in the far right lane. When they finally realized I'd changed lanes, Franklin tried to get over, but there was a car next to them, which he came dangerously close to hitting. He frantically jerked the wheel back to the right just before reaching the barrels and cones of the construction area. Aside from almost side-swiping the car next to them and crashing into the barrels and cones, the Kochs nearly got rear-ended by the car behind them as they were forced onto the onramp to who knows where. I almost had heart failure as I watched the whole episode unfold in my rearview mirror.

I worry about my own safety, but I made a conscious decision to take on this run, and all the risks that come with it. If something should happen to me, I can accept it. Yet, if something were to happen to someone who was trying to help me, I'd be devastated. Thank the good Lord Franklin and Catherine (as well as the construction workers and all the drivers around them) made it through the ordeal without getting hurt (and without any dings or dents).

Keep in mind, it did take a good 30 minutes for the Kochs to find me. I now realize I should have given them the address in Wilmington in case we got split up ... or, at the very least, exchanged phone numbers with them, but that would have been too easy. As you're learning, I like to do things the hard way.

After sighs of relief and heartfelt greetings, I hopped into Franklin and Catherine's car and we headed out. By the time we got to Villanova and I started my run, it was after 1pm. With another 21+ mile day ahead of me, I was worried that I might not get back to my car before dark. I was also worried about the Kochs getting home safely. I think it's safe to say their old hearts had enough stress for one day. I know mine did.

The day's run took me down more narrow, winding roads through woodland and past reservoirs and creeks. It was both tranquil and scenic, though I wasn't feeling it. After the frustrations of last night and the stress of this morning, my nerves were frayed, and I was spent.

A little way into it, my right hip started to tighten up and felt like it was pulling. During my training, I suffered an injury to my right hip, which put me out of commission for about two months. Truth be told, I almost cancelled the run because of it. The very thought that I might have aggravated it, coupled with everything else that had transpired, had me extremely worried and at one of my lowest points yet.

Al DeCesaris

Later in the day, a high school kid ran past me like I was standing still. I tried to keep up, but it was a futile effort. Within a few minutes, he was so far ahead of me I lost sight of him. Now I realize he's about 25 years younger than me, but I still found it demoralizing. After feeling sorry for myself, I remembered Aesop's fable *The Tortoise and the Hare*. Sure, the hare was much faster, but it was the tortoise that ultimately won the race. *Slow and steady wins the race*, I reminded myself.

Just after 5pm I reached Delaware, also known as "The First State" since it was the first of the 13 colonies to ratify the Constitution. I had spent four and a half fun-filled years there as an undergraduate at the University of Delaware and four more as manager of the Brickyard Tavern & Grill. Although most of my friends from those days have since moved away, there are still a few around; two of which would be my hosts this evening.

Soon after crossing the state line, I reached my car and ended one of the most mentally difficult days of the run. I then drove to the home of former Brickyard employees and good friends, Megan Panuska and her cousin Adrienne McDonald. Upon arrival, I was welcomed with open arms and pampered and fed. The problems and frustrations of the day were soon in the rearview mirror ... along with the Koch's near-death experience. It's amazing what the company of good friends can do for one's spirits.

146

Day 39 (10/16/14): Wilmington, DE to Elkton, MD [20.7 miles]

Yesterday it rained on and off most of the day. As far as I was concerned, the timing couldn't have been better. I'd run 10 straight days and needed a break. Plus, with my hip acting up, it was important to have time to recuperate. As an added bonus, I got to do my resting and recuperating in a nice hotel. (Will had come through again, booking me a room at a Marriott for two nights.) Ah, it's good to have generous friends.

This morning, I drove to the University of Delaware for an interview with Artika Casini for the *Messenger,* the school's alumni magazine. It was a great opportunity to raise awareness about Sturge-Weber syndrome with fellow alumni. After the interview, one of the university's photographers snapped pictures of me in my bright blue and yellow UD shirt. It didn't match my red shorts (actually it clashed terribly with it), but it was fitting for the occasion.

I then drove to the day's ending point, a roadside restaurant and bar on Route 273 in Elkton, Maryland called Wesley's. It's only about seven miles from downtown Newark, but in all my years living in Newark I'd never been there. And I had no idea how rural the

Al DeCesaris

area is or that there's a roadside bar out there. It's like a different world, one overrun by cornfields.

Adrienne was kind enough (and sly enough) to sneak out of work and come pick me up. She's lived in the area all of her life, and even she didn't know about this place. After having a few laughs about it, she drove me to the spot in Wilmington where I last left off. It was great to see her one more time even if only for a short while.

It was just before 1pm when I got started. With 20+ miles to cover and a 6:24pm sunset, I needed to maintain a steady pace and keep the breaks to a minimum. I hoped my hip was up for it because if it wasn't and I had to walk, even for a little while, I might end up out on that rural stretch of Route 273 after dark.

Thank goodness, that wasn't the case. There was some lingering discomfort, but nothing to complain about (and that's saying something coming from me).

The late start wasn't an issue either. I was out of Wilmington and moving toward Newark before I knew it. Some days I just move better than others. No doubt, a day of rest helps, and crossing a state line always gives me a boost. But what had me pumped up most was the anticipation of running through my old college town. It sounds corny, but I'm a nostalgic guy, and Newark reminds me of some of the best times with some of the best people I know.

Another thing that had me feeling upbeat was knowing that tomorrow I was going to see family and friends at a fundraiser in Towson, Maryland. We were expecting a good turnout including my immediate family,

Dr. Anne Comi, and Paul Siegel. I only wish I had the opportunity to meet with more Sturge-Weber syndrome patients like Paul during the run. However, coordinating such meetings is difficult since I'm by myself (and on foot) and uncertain of how far I'll be able to go each day.

Just before 4pm I reached Newark, turned onto Main Street, and began my trip down memory lane. I ran past the old establishments I frequented and the new ones that have sprung up since I left. I then came to the Main Street Galleria and looked up at the location where the Brickyard Tavern & Grill once resided. The place now goes by a different name and has a much different look ... as does a lot of what I saw. As strange as it all seemed, there were still many things about Main Street that rang true. And I was glad to have this place, that held so many great memories for me, become a part of this grand new one.

About two miles past Newark proper, I spotted a sign that read, "Maryland Welcomes You. Enjoy Your Visit!" I was again overcome with a wave of emotions, albeit very different ones. Though this wasn't a part of the state I was familiar with, Maryland *is* my home state and reaching it was a significant achievement. It was my ninth state and the last one before I reached "the South." After "The Old Line State," as Maryland is known, it's all downhill.

As I finished out the day, my heels started to hurt. It didn't help that there were some major hills between the state line and Wesley's. One in particular was one of the

Al DeCesaris

biggest I'd faced thus far. Funny, those hills didn't seem so big when I drove them.

That night I had dinner with Chris Peters, another former Brickyard employee and friend of roughly 17 years. Chris and I hadn't seen each other in some time; but have stayed in touch. Still, there's nothing like catching up with an old friend in person. And there's nothing like being told by that old friend, that tomorrow you'll have a running partner.

Day 40 (10/17/14): Elkton, MD to Darlington, MD [20.9 miles]

Chris and I met at Harvey's Jr. (a roadside restaurant and bar similar to Wesley's) in Darlington at 7:30am (I was actually 20 minutes late, but darn if I didn't try to be on time). After we put together a detailed plan (which basically consisted of running 20.9 miles as fast as we could), Chris hopped in my car and we drove to Wesley's.

As we made our way there, I noticed how hilly the terrain was between the starting and ending points. I also noticed that, like the end of yesterday's run, the landscape was dominated by farmland. Hills and mundane scenery usually result in boring, challenging runs. However, today the weather was fantastic, and I had company. Since I began, I hadn't had anyone run with me an entire day. Chris would be the first. And I couldn't think of a more determined person to tackle a long day of running hills with than my old friend.

The road was straight and the shoulder wide, allowing us to run side by side. As we passed farm after farm, we talked about the challenges I've been facing since I set out and the ones he's been facing as of late. This September marked the one-year anniversary of Chris' sobriety. I wasn't aware he had a problem with alcohol, but upon learning of it, I couldn't have been prouder of him for having the courage to face it.

In his fight against his addiction, Chris employs the same philosophy he uses to accomplish his goals in the gym (which, judging from the pace he was keeping, he's doing an amazing job). It's based on the acronym DFQ, which according to Chris stands for, "Don't F*ing Quit!" When he feels even a twinge of temptation or gets fatigued in the gym, Chris tells himself "DFQ." No matter how hard it gets, no matter how painful it is, no matter how much he wants to give in or give up, that unyielding and perseverant mindset helps him fight through.

There's a famous quote attributed to Mahatma Gandhi that seems written for Chris. "Strength does not come from winning. Your struggles develop your strengths. When you go through hardships and decide not to surrender, that is strength." Reflecting on those words and seeing proof of that strength in my old friend, gives me hope for myself and for Jenna. Even though I've overcome a number of difficult challenges, I'm still not even halfway through my run. Without a doubt, I'll face more and possibly greater challenges. Jenna, in her young life, has suffered far more hardships than most will experience in a lifetime, and undoubtedly will encounter many more. Knowing that those experiences help us develop strength makes me hopeful that our adversities can be overcome.

Just after 11am, Chris and I reached the Conowingo Bridge Dam. It had one lane going in each direction with 18-inch-wide shoulders sandwiched between concrete barriers. After a powwow and pep-talk, we set out with a heaping helping of caution. It was to be single file running the length of the one-mile-long bridge ... that was until we got three-quarters of the way across, where the road construction began.

Keep in mind, we came this way because this was the only pedestrian-friendly bridge that crossed the Susquehanna River close to my route. How exactly this is considered a pedestrian-friendly bridge, I'll never know. As far as I'm concerned, the Conowingo Bridge Dam is 100% pedestrian *unfriendly*, sadistically so. Chris thought so too. And judging from the reactions of the people who drove past us, they agreed as well. One guy even yelled out his window, "you're f*ing crazy," which, for running on this bridge, we undoubtedly were.

As you know, I'm a slow runner. Yet, as I crossed the bridge, I ran so fast I think I could have qualified for the Olympics. The only one faster than me, other than Usain Bolt, was Chris. Thank goodness he was with me because when we came to the construction area, it was his encouragement that made all the difference. Through that area the concrete barriers pinched in, forcing us to cross to the other side of the road and run *with* traffic. The rest of the way it was a panic-stricken sprint. Chris got across first and turned to spur me on. Although I didn't realize it at the time, he later told me there was a huge camper coming up behind me as I covered the final stretch. By the grace of God, I made it across safely, but it was close, *very* close.

Al DeCesaris

We ended up reaching Harvey's Jr. in record time. Well, maybe it wasn't record time for Chris, but it was for me. As we were readying to drive back, Chris went into the trunk of his car to get some water. Yet, when he closed it, he locked his keys inside. Yep, that really happened. After about an hour of trying to unlock the car with a coat hanger, a sweet lady from Harvey's Jr. named Lois gave us a ride back to Wesley's. Chris' stepfather Brian met us there with another set of keys. Although we could have done without all the drama, it was great to meet Brian and did make for a good laugh (at Chris's expense, of course). Teasing aside, it was awesome of Chris to take the time and put forth the effort to support me and the cause the way he did.

I then drove to the home of Theresa and Dave Brulinski. They're great friends of my sister Ida and her husband Ed and are hosting me for the night. After catching up with them and sharing stories from my run (which now include the "locking the keys in the car" fiasco), I got cleaned up and headed to the Greene Turtle in Towson for the fundraiser.

It was a fun night with a great group of people, which included in addition to the Brulinskis, my family, Paul Siegel, Dr. Anne Comi and her family, and many others. After so many long, difficult, and lonely days on the road, the run today with Chris and the night's festivities with dear friends and loved ones were wonderful experiences for which I will forever be grateful.

Day 41 (10/18/14): Darlington, MD to Carney, MD [23.9 miles]

The day started with a big breakfast including freshly laid eggs from the Brulinski's chicken coop (no joke, they have an actual chicken coop in their backyard). After a leisurely morning, I followed Dave to The Barn in Carney. Back in the day, The Barn was a hot spot for 20-somethings and one of Dave and Theresa's favorite watering holes. When I went inside to see if it was okay to leave my car there, Dave came in with me to have a look. I'm not sure what the place was like when they frequented it, but it smelled like a fraternity house now. According to Dave, not much had changed.

He then drove me back to Harvey's Jr. in Darlington. It was funny watching his reaction when I got out of the car and started off. I'm not sure what was going through his head, but he seemed uncomfortable just leaving me there. I guess it is strange leaving someone you know on the side of the road in the middle of nowhere and just driving away.

It was close to 1pm when I got started. I suppose my leisurely morning was a bit too leisurely. It wouldn't have been a big deal had it been a normal day (whatever that means when you're running down the entire East

Al DeCesaris

Coast). Yet, today I was to run roughly 24 miles, the most I'd run to date.

Not far into my run, I realized I'd eaten too much or maybe not given my food enough time to digest. Whatever the case, I felt sick to my stomach. As I was struggling down the road, I belched and threw up in my mouth. I know people joke about that kind of thing, but as embarrassed as I am to admit it, it happened. I literally vomited in my mouth. Food for thought (bad pun intended), digest your food before setting out on a 23.9-mile run. You should probably digest your food before setting out on a run of any distance.

It was more rural running today: woodland and farmland, farmland and woodland, on and on. Adding to the excitement of the day was a flying acorn. Seriously, at one point an acorn hit me in the calf so hard it felt like it had been shot out of a BB gun. Worse yet was the wind. I'm not sure how fast it was gusting; but moving against it was like running with a parachute on my back. Believe it or not, some athletes actually train like that. Talk about gluttons for punishment. And that's coming from the guy who's running through 14-states over 3-months down the entire East Coast. Despite the gusting wind, the projectile acorn, and the mouthful of vomit, the sun was shining, which kept my spirits up.

Later in the day, a song by the band Blue October came on that reminded me of friends and relationships long past. I told you before I'm a sentimental guy. I'm also a huge music enthusiast and can get lost in the right song. As the tempo picked up, I got into a zone and started picking up the pace. Before I knew it, I was running down the road at full sprint. At one point my visor flew off my head, and I snagged it out of the air without breaking stride. And just as the song reached its crescendo, I scaled a big hill like I was Rocky scaling the steps of the Philadelphia Museum of Art. I think it's safe to say, this is one of those songs I can get lost in … come to think of it, the main track from *Rocky* is one of those songs too.

As the day wore on, I found myself running through dense woodland on a hilly stretch of road that had a 6-inch-wide shoulder bordered by a metal guardrail, which I was none too happy about it. I can do without the daily dose of high-stress running. However, the road did take me past the picturesque Gunpowder Falls and some magnificent historic homes.

The road then straightened and widened. Before long, I emerged from the rural back roads of the countryside to the congested suburban ones of Carney. A mile or so later, I spotted my destination and not a minute too soon. The sun was just about to set.

As I trotted into the The Barn's parking lot, I reveled in my achievement. I had just completed a 23.9-mile run and set a new record high … and only puked once while doing it. Had I not been in the midst of this 2,000-some-odd mile epic journey, I may have gone inside The Barn for a celebratory drink. I'm sure Dave and Theresa would have gotten a kick out of that. But, after all those miles (and lots more to come), I needed a cold Gatorade a lot more than I needed a cold beer.

Running The Coast For A Cure

there, but seeing it got me interested to check out the campus. Today, however, was not the day. It was already 2:30pm, and I still had another 15 miles to cover before dark.

I entered the second address into Google Maps and started off. It was pretty much a straight shot into the heart of the city, though I did adjust the route a little to see Mt. Vernon. It's one of the city's oldest neighborhoods and at one time was home to some of its wealthiest residents. It derives its name from George Washington's home in Virginia, and in its main square is a monument dedicated to our first president. It's one of my favorite places in the city, so I made sure to stop by for a visit.

I also used the pit stop to rest my right foot. On the approach to Mt. Vernon, I had developed discomfort in my right heel, which soon escalated to intense pain. It was the third day in a row wearing the Hokas, which may have been the problem. From what I've been told, shoes need recovery time so the foam in the soles can decompress. Who knows if that's actually true? More likely, I had just worn them out. They did have about 350 miles on them.

The next stop was the Inner Harbor. It's a well-known tourist area with shops, restaurants, hotels, the National Aquarium, and the Maryland Science Center situated around a historic seaport. After taking in the sights and sounds of the Inner Harbor, I entered the third address into Google Maps and continued on.

Al DeCesaris

I ran past Camden Yards (home of MLB's Orioles) just as the crowds started pouring out of the adjacent M&T Stadium (home of the NFL's Ravens). Sometimes I forget which day of the week it is (they all seem to run together), but the football fans, decked out in their black and purple Ravens' gear, reminded me it was a Sunday. They also reminded me how annoying drunk football fans can be, especially when you get heckled by them. I figured the Ravens must have lost the game and their fans were venting their frustrations; but come to find out they had won. I suppose the red shirt I wore made them think I was a fan of the opposing team ... or maybe that's just how Ravens fans normally behave.

Whatever the case, I was soon a safe distance from the hecklers and making my way out of the city and into the suburbs. The final stretch put me back on Route 1. It also had me running up and down a bunch of big hills. With my right heel hurting the way it was, I decided that today's run would be the Hokas' swan song.

Around 6pm, I reached my destination in Elkridge. I then drove to my parents' house outside of Annapolis and enjoyed a home-cooked meal with my family. It was a great way to end the day, especially so because my little inspiration, Jenna, was there with me, proudly wearing her new *Running The Coast For A Cure* shirt with a big smile on her face.

Day 43 (10/20/14): Elkridge, MD to Washington, D.C. [25.2 miles]

After a big breakfast and a large cup of joe, my mom drove me to the gas station/convenience store where I left off. She was also going to pick me up later at the day's ending point in Washington, D.C. I can't stress enough how much having someone drop me off and pick me up helps. It not only cuts out the stress and aggravation of having to find rides and move my car, but it saves time, which this morning allowed me to sleep in.

The weather today was cool and breezy. So, I wore my white long-sleeve mock turtleneck as a base-layer (as of late I've been wearing it more days than not). On top of it, I wore my new *Running The Coast For A Cure* navy short-sleeved shirt with the event logo emblazoned on the front. I wanted to have it from the very beginning of the run, but I didn't place the order in time (I did have a few other things to worry about, you know).

The route for the day was about as straight forward as it could get. Days like this (when I don't have to worry about moving my car, finding rides, and navigating confusing directions) don't come often, but when they do it allows me to focus on the actual run, which is more than enough to worry about.

Al DeCesaris

It also helped that I was wearing one of the new pairs of Brooks Glycerin running shoes that had been donated by Charm City Run in Annapolis (thank you to the Maryland-based running store for their generosity). It only took a few miles for me to realize that the new shoes made a huge difference. The heel pain I'd felt yesterday wasn't even noticeable. Although I had 25.2 miles to cover (my longest day yet), I felt confident that with the help of my comfy new kicks, I could handle it.

Whether it was the new shoes or not having to worry about looking at Google Maps every five minutes, I moved well and made great time. At times like these, I have to remind myself to slow down, otherwise I'll just end up reaching my ending point before my ride does. As one of my law school professors once said of the three-year law school experience, "it's a marathon, not a sprint." For me, in the midst of this journey, that sentiment rings true. The highs and lows of it (both physically and mentally) need to be kept in check.

Around 2pm, I ran through the city of College Park and past the University of Maryland. About 45 minutes later, I found myself crossing out of my home state and into our nation's capital. Reaching Washington, D.C. was another banner achievement. It was the city I was born in and where I spent a good portion of my adult life.

After snapping my ceremonial selfie and texting friends and family (you know me, I like to keep my peeps in the loop), I continued on. At the D.C. line, Route 1 becomes Rhode Island Avenue. I followed it across Northeast D.C. into the Northwest quadrant of the city. I then turned onto 10th street and finished the run a few minutes later at the pickup point, Will Futch's condo.

Will was out of town, but he'd been nice enough to offer his place to me for the night. First, though, I needed to get back to Maryland to go to Jenna's soccer practice. I'd been invited by her soccer coach, Iain Goodwin, to speak to their team about my run. Anytime I'm asked to speak about my efforts to help those living with Sturge-Weber syndrome, I jump at the chance (figuratively not literally, of course).

When I arrived at Jenna's practice, I was greeted by Ida, Jenna, Kyle (Jenna's brother), Coach Iain, and Jenna's girlfriends Katie and Emmi. I soon realized that I wasn't just speaking to Jenna's team, but to all of the youth soccer teams at the park. Nothing like ratcheting up the pressure.

I spoke to the kids about my run and the benefits of staying fit (it seemed appropriate; I *was* at a soccer practice). I also made sure to focus on the value of helping those in need through charity work. In this crazy world we live in, teaching children positive lessons is of vital importance.

Afterward, the kids were told to run a lap around the fields, and I was asked to join them (as though 25.2 miles wasn't enough for one day). Not far into it a couple of kids asked why I was going so slow? I guess they were expecting something more from the guy running down the East Coast. "Because I'm old," I said with a laugh. I was also sore and tired. But the real reason was Jenna had fallen behind, and I didn't want to leave her.

By the time we were halfway around, Jenna was struggling, and her breathing was labored. She stopped running and began to walk. Soon we lost sight of the other kids and Jenna seemed despondent. It's times like these that I really notice how much Sturge-Weber syndrome adversely affects her. And I'm reminded just how difficult her life is, and how difficult it will be in the years to come. The thought of it breaks my heart.

Yet, I thank God Jenna is able to be here with her friends, participating in an activity that brings her joy. And I thank Him for people like Coach Iain and her friends Katie and Emmi who accept her for who she is. They don't need to be taught the importance of acceptance and helping others. They already know all about it and demonstrate it through their love for Jenna.

Day 44 (10/21/14): Washington, D.C. to Lorton, VA [21.2 miles]

In the morning, my parents met me at Will's condo to pick up my car. The plan was for them to drive it to the day's ending point, a gas station on Route 1 in Lorton, Virginia, and leave it there for me. It was a big help because after the day's run, I had to drive back to Maryland for another fundraising event at the Greene Turtle in Annapolis. If you're wondering why we didn't schedule this event a couple of days earlier when I was still in the Annapolis area … well, so am I.

Alan Faneca arrived not long after. As I mentioned before, he and his wife Julie have been ardent supporters of my family's efforts for years. When I did my bike ride, they arranged television and radio interviews in Pittsburgh. Alan even flew there to do the interviews with me to help spread the word. Well this time around they came up with another great way to support the cause — Alan would be joining me for today's run, all 21.2 miles of it. Talk about going the extra mile! Silly pun aside, I couldn't be more appreciative of everything the Fanecas have done and was thrilled to have Alan running with me.

The beginning of the run took us through downtown D.C. with its high-rise buildings of glass, steel, brick, and

Al DeCesaris

stone. We then turned onto 14th street, which we followed past Pennsylvania Avenue and the White House (just blocks away) and onto the National Mall. From there, we could see the museums of the Smithsonian Institution and the U.S. Capital. We also had a fantastic view of the Washington Monument.

Like the one in Baltimore, the Monument commemorates our first President, George Washington. It was designed by the same architect, Robert Mills, though the two are very different. The one in D.C. is reminiscent of an Egyptian obelisk and stands at a towering 554 feet, making it the tallest stone structure in the world.

A few minutes later, we reached the Tidal Basin, and were treated to stunning views of the Jefferson Memorial. It's an open-air Neoclassical structure with a portico at the entrance, a colonnade of Ionic columns around its circular perimeter, and a dome above a 19-foot-tall bronze statue of Thomas Jefferson, American Founding Father, principal author of the *Declaration of Independence*, and third President of the United States.

We crossed the 14th Street/George Mason Memorial Bridge over the Potomac River and entered the Commonwealth of Virginia. Another interesting history fact: eight U.S. presidents were born in Virginia, that's more than any other state. Thus, it stands to reason that one of Virginia's nicknames is "Mother of Presidents."

However, Virginia isn't the "Mother of Signs." When Alan and I stepped foot in the Commonwealth, there was no sign to welcome us (or if there was, it was so

Running The Coast For A Cure

small we didn't see it). Either way, I was short one state-sign-selfie, and not the least bit happy about it.

Our route then took us down the Mt. Vernon Trail. The trail is a nearly 18-mile-long pedestrian and bicycle path that follows the shoreline of the Potomac River all the way to George Washington's estate at Mt. Vernon. We weren't on it that long, but we did take it past Ronald Reagan Washington National Airport and through Old Town Alexandria.

Old Town is a historic district with colonial and Federal-style buildings and cobblestone streets. It was once a major seaport and was even part of the original U.S. capital, though it was later retroceded to Virginia. Today the streets are lined with restaurants, boutiques, shops, and theaters, making it a popular destination for tourists and locals alike.

Like yesterday, I wore another new pair of Brooks Glycerin running shoes compliments of Charm City Run. And like yesterday, I was running well and without pain. Alan was moving well too. However, he didn't need a new pair of shoes to do it. He's a former offensive lineman who played 13 seasons in the NFL. During his time in the league, he was named to the All-Pro Team and the Pro Bowl nine times and won a Super Bowl with the Pittsburgh Steelers. Since his NFL days, Alan has taken up marathon running. So, he *definitely* doesn't need a new pair of shoes the way I do.

Toward the end of the run, we faced a few big climbs. They weren't fun, but knowing we were almost done made them tolerable. As we crested the last hill, I caught sight of the gas station in Lorton where my parents left my car. Minutes later, we were there congratulating each other on a successful run for a worthwhile cause and two beautiful little girls near and dear to our hearts.

After dropping Alan off at his house and thanking him for his enthusiastic support, I drove to my parents' house to get cleaned up. Soon after, I was at the Greene Turtle enjoying a fun and relaxing evening. The benefit of these restaurant fundraisers, aside from getting to spend time with family and friends, is that a percentage of each guest check is donated to the cause, which in turn is used to fund Sturge-Weber syndrome research. So, the more we eat, the more money we raise. Suffice to say, after running 134 miles in the past six days, I had an appetite big enough to raise a boat-load of cash all by myself.

Al DeCesaris, Jenna Heck, and Ida Heck in Annapolis, Maryland
(photo courtesy of Bob Melamud).

Day 46 (10/23/14): Lorton, VA to Stafford, VA [23.9 miles]

I woke to bacon and eggs and my first ever cup of Bulletproof Coffee. It's coffee blended with coconut oil and butter. It sounds fattening and artery-clogging, but it's actually a fat loss, muscle building, energy boosting drink (or so they say). It was tasty, if nothing else.

As I ate breakfast and sipped my "uber-healthy" cup of joe, I chatted with Alan, Julie, and their son Burtie. I also got to spend time with Julie's father, who I met at dinner last night. It had rained yesterday, so I took the day off (resting most of it) and spent the evening with the Fanecas. Like last night, it was a relaxing morning in the company of great people. The only one missing was Anabelle. She had headed off to school before I woke up. I was sorry to have missed her, though I did get to spend some quality time with her at dinner last night.

After breakfast, I said my goodbyes to Julie. From the moment I arrived, she and Alan made me feel at home and like a part of their family. They're amazing people. And their love for their children and their ongoing efforts to improve the quality of life of those living with Sturge-Weber syndrome is extraordinary.

Alan and Burtie followed me to the Log Cabin Restaurant in Stafford, the day's ending point. I parked

Al DeCesaris

my car there, got into Alan's vehicle, and we headed to the gas station in Lorton where we left off. The Faneca men then wished me well, and I started down Route 1 for 23.9 miles of hilly running.

Not long into it, I came to an area with construction on both sides of the road. It created a real dilemma and left me with two options, neither of which were good. I could either run in the dirt and mud of the construction site among heavy machinery or run on the busy road hugging the concrete barriers to avoid speeding vehicles. After some internal debate, I decided to run on the road. I figured if I ran quick enough, I'd be able to get past the areas where the concrete barriers narrowed the roadway before any vehicles came by. Well, my "quick running" turned into a full-on nervous sprint. Thank heavens, I made it past the barriers *just* before a wave of traffic flew by. Next construction site I think I'll opt to stay behind the "protective" barriers. You'd think I would have learned that lesson by now.

Later, I ran past MCB Quantico, one of the largest U.S. Marine Corps bases in the world. Also, on the base are the training academies of the U.S. Drug Enforcement Administration and the Federal Bureau of Investigation as well as the headquarters of the Naval Criminal Investigative Service ... that's DEA, FBI, and NCIS for those who prefer the agencies' cool acronyms.

Afterward, I found myself on a stretch of road with an uneven and eroding shoulder covered with large rocks. I had to watch each step for fear of tripping or turning an ankle. I had come across rugged terrain before, but this

Running The Coast For A Cure

made even trail running seem like child's play. I only had to suffer through it a couple of miles before Deputy Nick Torrice pulled up to give me a police escort.

This wasn't just by chance, mind you. When Sergeant Reed of the Stafford County Police Department heard I was coming through the area, he offered to have a deputy escort me to my destination. So, for the last nine miles or so, I got to run in the right lane of Route 1 with a police patrol car trailing behind. As I made my way down the road, I received encouragement in the form of thumbs ups, cheering, clapping ... and a few curious stares as well.

Although Deputy Torrice didn't need me to run at any particular pace, I found myself running much faster than I normally do. I don't know if it was the result of adrenaline or the memory of Officer Steve from Maine forcing me to sprint down the road, but I made great time despite lots of big hills. When I reached the Log Cabin Restaurant, Deputy Torrice congratulated me on a good run. It was one of my fastest runs. I'm glad someone was there to witness it.

I then drove to the Stanger's vacation home on Lake Anna. My childhood friend Bob and his wife Kimmie have been incredible supporters of our efforts from the start and offered to host me for a couple of days. The plan was for Bob to shuttle me to and from my starting and ending points and even do a little running with me. It was a long day. But starting it and ending it in the company of such amazing friends (and having an *injury-free* police escort in between) made it a special one.

173

Day 47 (10/24/14): Stafford, VA to Woodford, VA [20.6 miles]

Give me a couple extra hours of sleep and I'm loving life (or, more accurately, not a grumpy S.O.B.). And it hasn't just been this way during the run. Since I was kid, I've needed more sleep than your average Joe: a fact that my *brother* Joe has always been eager to point out to anyone who would listen. Seriously though, sleep has always been the cure-all for me. It even worked its magic on that now infamous blister I neglected to mention.

Over the past few days, I'd developed a painful blister on the big toe of my right foot. I ignored it at first. And as it grew, I ignored it even more, hoping it would go away on its own. Well, last night when I saw Bob's reaction to it, I couldn't ignore it any longer. It had become the blister of all blisters – the size of a cherry (it had the look of one too). How I ran with that thing, I'll never know. Lucky for me, Bob had a straight pin and a bottle of hydrogen peroxide in the house. After the "surgical session" and a long night of sleep, the blister was gone and my toe on the mend. Still, it might be a while before I take my shoes and socks off in front of anyone.

After breakfast, Bob drove me back to the Log Cabin Restaurant in Stafford. Today's plan was to continue

Al DeCesaris

south on Route 1 to Elliott's Auto Service in Woodford. If all went well (i.e. if Bob got his work done in time), he'd park his car there, then meet me a few miles down the road and run those last miles of the day with me.

Weather-wise it was a nice day for a run. The sun was shining and there was a light breeze. However, not far into it, my right shoulder and upper back started to hurt. I wondered if the pain was caused by the weight of the hydration pack or from carrying my cell phone in my right hand. I realize that running hours on end every day with a cell phone in your hand is a bit foolish, but come on, I *have to* DJ my music. And I've got to be able to screen my calls in case it's a telemarketer or worse yet, an ex-girlfriend.

Around 2pm, I ran over a bridge spanning the Rappahannock River. The river crosses the northern part of Virginia from the Blue Ridge Mountains to the Chesapeake Bay. On the south side of the river is Fredericksburg. Even though the city was easy to navigate, my pace was pathetic. This was the result of all the traffic lights and my shoulder and back pain, plus stomach issues (that's code for I needed to go to the bathroom). Good thing there were plenty of fast food restaurants around; otherwise I would have been up sh*ts creek.

When I got beyond the city, I started moving at a respectable pace. Yet, just as I started making decent progress, my cell phone went dead. It wasn't a big deal, but it forced me to stop and take off my hydration pack so I could retrieve my charger (without Google Maps

Running The Coast For A Cure

and my compass app I'm lost, literally). It was the story of the day. Every time I got a little momentum going, something or the other would break my rhythm.

On days like this, I realize the importance of being persistent. Most undertakings, especially ones this ambitious, come with numerous challenges and setbacks. Lord knows I've experienced my fair share, and I'm still not even halfway through. I would image there will be plenty more. To overcome them and make it to the promised land (AKA Key Largo, Florida), persistence is key.

Not long after, back-to-back drivers put my persistence to the test. As I ran down Route 1, I spotted a hitchhiker a few hundred yard ahead on the same side of the road as me. I'm not sure what the deal was, but the sight of this guy seemed to distract drivers. It was as though they'd never seen a hitchhiker before. (Who knows, maybe they hadn't. We are a *long* way from Maine.) Still, why that made the oncoming cars veer toward the white line as they drove past me, I haven't a clue. Whatever the reason, I nearly got hit, not once but twice.

I'm happy to report the day ended on a high note. About five miles from the ending point, I hit my stride and found myself running at a startling pace. Even Bob was impressed by how fast I was moving (that's because he knows how slow of a runner I actually am). Those might have been some of my best miles yet. And running the last few with one of my childhood – and present day – best friends, made them all the better.

177

Day 48 (10/25/14): Woodford, VA to Montpelier, VA [22.3 miles]

U nlike yesterday, there was no sleeping in this morning. Bob had to be back in Maryland for his son's soccer game, so we had to get going early if he was to make it there in time. Our first stop was Conwell's Auto Service in Montpelier where I was to end the day's run. It was closed so I just parked my car in their parking lot and hoped it would be there when I finished. I then hopped in Bob's car and we rode back to Elliott's Auto Service in Woodford where I left off yesterday.

It was awesome of Bob to host me, and to join me yesterday out on the road. Our run together, coupled with the two days we cycled together during my bike ride, makes Bob the only person to put in miles with me during both charity events.

After saying our goodbyes, Bob headed north on route 1 and I headed south. It was a crisp 45 degrees, making it one of the coldest days yet. Some people swear by it, but I hate running in the cold. The one comfort I had was later in the day the temperature was expected to climb into the high 60s. Those warm temps couldn't come soon enough.

About 20 minutes into it, I left Route 1 for narrow and winding country roads. This wasn't by choice, mind you.

Al DeCesaris

If I had my druthers, I would have stayed on Route 1 with its cars and convenience stores (i.e. civilization) the entire day. Yet, as you know, Google Maps' walking route charts my course, so into the backwoods I went. Keep in mind, the woodland and farmland I ran through were scenic. If I had company, I might have enjoyed it. However, it was just me out there, and these rural lands had me feeling isolated and alone.

In addition, my right shoulder and back were acting up again. What had started as discomfort and a fleeting worry had escalated into pain and legitimate concern. I didn't know what to do about it, but I could start by getting my cell phone out of my hand while I ran. In the front of my hydration pack are pockets big enough to hold a phone and that's where mine belongs.

Some days are just harder than others. If you couldn't tell, this was "one of those days." Physically I was cold, tired, and in pain, and mentally I was in the dumps.

As I lumbered down those desolate country roads, the discomfort and pain preoccupied my thoughts. After a while, that negativity gained power and I started questioning what I was doing out there. The anxiety that came with it soon became so overwhelming, I stopped running and walked off the road. I suppose some of that could be attributed to the fact that I'd just spent time with family and friends and was alone again. Regardless of the reasons, my will was fading.

I didn't know what to do so I called my sister. "What's the point of all this?" I asked, though it was more a statement of frustration than a question. I can't

180

remember Ida's exact words, but she basically told me, what I'm doing matters to her and, more importantly, it matters to Jenna. She went on to say, Jenna is super excited about my run, and that I *have* to finish it for *her*.

That's all I needed to hear. The happiness and well-being of Jenna, and of all those with Sturge-Weber syndrome, is what this charity run is all about. With that in mind, I set the doubt and frustration aside and got back to the job at hand.

In addition to Ida's pep talk, a little extra motivation came in the form of four attacking dogs. For the record, these weren't friendly pooches looking to play. These were berserk canines looking for blood. Lucky for me (and for them), their owner called them off just before things got out of hand. And, by out of hand, I mean just before someone got bit … or four other someones (of the four-legged variety) got sprayed with mace.

Just after 2pm, I reached my ending point. Thank goodness, my car was still there because a construction crew was on site repaving the parking lot. Although they hadn't gotten to the section where my car was parked, *yet*, I'd imagine a call for a tow truck had already been placed. What an end to the day that would have been.

Like I said before, this was one of those "harder" days, maybe one of the hardest. Even so, days like this help put things in perspective and teach valuable lessons. For me, this day reminded me what the run is all about and what *truly* matters.

Day 49 (10/26/14): Montpelier, VA to Powhatan, VA [25.1 miles]

After getting up at the crack of dawn yesterday, this morning I made sure to get some extra sleep. It was much needed, as was a big breakfast. Lucky for me, the hotel where I'm staying (another room courtesy of Will Futch) served complimentary breakfast. I'm not sure how much the room cost, but I think it's safe to say that with all the food I ate, I got Will's money's worth.

Today I'd top 25 miles for only the second time and wanted to make sure I was prepared for the rigors of the long day. I started as I always do by going through my pre-run checklist. After taking care of the basics, I got to the serious stuff, like rolling out my stiff legs on my foam roller. For those who have never done it, it's no joke. It's agonizing (at least when I do it), but it's also one of the best ways to loosen up your hamstrings, quadriceps, and IT bands. After suffering through it, I headed out to meet my volunteer drivers.

The two brave souls who had volunteered to drive me and deal with my tired and cranky (and at times, smelly) self, were none other than my parents. Yep, mom and dad had answered the call when no other drivers could be found. It was great to have them here with me, and not just because I wouldn't have to worry about finding rides, though that would make life easier. It was the opportunity to share this experience with the two people who supported me most.

Without my parents' support, this run wouldn't be going as well as it is (which is funny to say because it hasn't exactly been the smoothest operation). In fact, if not for my parents, it probably never would have gotten off the ground. Since the day this nutty idea became a bona fide charity event, my mom has logged countless hours on planning and logistics while my dad has handled media outreach and procured sponsorships. Now, with them shuttling me around for the next few days, they'd be experiencing this thing with me, in all its insanely awesome glory.

As they drove me back to yesterday's ending point, I saw some of the terrain I was to cover and realized today's run, like the previous few, was going to be another scenic one. With all its unspoiled land, waterways, and rolling hills, this part of Virginia is gorgeous, and the autumn colors only added to its beauty. Obviously, I was feeling a bit more optimistic today. Sunshine, temps in the high 60s, and having your two biggest fans with you will do that for you.

The early part of the run was quiet and peaceful taking me past fields and farms. In the afternoon, the road wound through a wooded area with tall leafy trees bordering the roadway and forming a canopy overhead. Although the sun shone brightly, along this stretch it was veiled and gave the leaves an iridescent glow.

Running The Coast For A Cure

As I made my way down one narrow, shoulder-less country road then the next (if you haven't noticed, it's all country roads these days), I straddled the outside white line and hoped oncoming vehicles could see me. I soon realized there was no problem with drivers seeing me; it was that many of them were angry I was there. *How do I keep ending up in situations like this?* I will say, some motorists were supportive – giving me a wide berth, a nod of the head, or a thumbs-up as they drove by. Most, however, were downright nasty. I got venomous glares, wagging fingers, and one driver even tried to run me off the road. No, that's not an exaggeration, though I wish it was. This maniac actually veered his truck toward me just as he closed in, forcing me into the tall grass on the side of the road. And for good measure, he gave me the death stare as he flew by me.

By day's end, I was exhausted and irritated. Running 25 miles and almost getting run over will do that to you. My parents had seen a bit of what I faced as they drove to the pickup point. They couldn't believe how nerve-racking and dangerous these runs can be. My dad said, "no one could understand it unless they saw it for themselves." I agree with that to some extent, though to truly understand it you need to get out there and run the miles among these maniacs. This is nothing like an organized run with designated (and safe) running areas lined with supporters cheering you on. This is hard, lonely, and often times dangerous work that needs to be done again and again until I reach Key Largo … or until I become someone's hood ornament.

Running The Coast For A Cure

bunch of stomach-churning episodes, but this might have been the worst yet.

Later in the day, my right knee started hurting. A knee injury, as I stressed before, is something that has always worried me. I feel it's one of those injuries you can't just power through like you can others. So, in an effort to protect it, I made various adjustments to my form. It seemed to work in lessening the pressure, but after a while my right hamstring started to bother me. Whether that was the result of the adjustments or just coincidence, I wasn't certain. What I did know was that I now had a new problem brewing.

A few miles later, the discomfort in my hamstring began to intensify. And it was further exacerbated by the hilly terrain I had to deal with the last few miles of the day. By the time I reached my ending point, I was in considerable pain.

That evening I put a call into all three members of my medical team to get their thoughts on my hamstring issue (notice how I'm not saying injury). I realize calling one of them would have been sufficient. Each of these guys is at the top of their profession. Still, I feared I had a real problem, and I was hoping one of them would give me positive news. To my disappointment, the prognosis I received from each of them was the same – it's a hamstring strain. Short of taking time off, I'm left to the usual self-administered treatments. Well, I'm not interested in taking time off (at least not any time soon). I'll just treat the "injury" as best I can and do what I can to deal with the pain, and the area's malevolent drivers.

189

Day 51 (10/28/14): Amelia Court House, VA to Blackstone, VA [22.7 miles]

As I walked through the motel lobby in my running apparel ready to start another day, the front desk clerk looked on in utter disbelief. He had seen me limp in yesterday evening like a decrepit old man and was so concerned he suggested I get examined by a doctor. I'm sure my bum hamstring wasn't helping matters, but the reality is – that's pretty much how I look at the end of all my runs. My muscles tighten up as soon as I finish, making walking even a short distance (like from the car through the motel lobby) a struggle.

When I see this kind of reaction it makes me reflect on the extreme nature of what I'm doing. I'm running on average 20+ miles a day and plan to do it for three consecutive months down the entire East Coast. When I think about it in those terms (and acknowledge everything I'm putting my body through), a reaction like his makes perfect sense, even if the pain and stress I'm subjecting my body to doesn't.

Speaking of which, with my right hamstring being a concern, I made sure to wrap it. It wasn't anything fancy, just an athletic bandage my parents picked up at a local pharmacy. But I figured it should support and stabilize the muscles and reduce the chance of further damage.

Al DeCesaris

The sun was out again today, and the temperature was in the high 70s. The only knock on the weather was the headwind. The resistance it created slowed my pace and hampered my progress. It also led to a lot of extra work, which quickly tired me out.

It was another day of desolate woodland and farmland. For a good portion of the day, it was just me, trees, crops, and cattle … and goats (I definitely don't want to leave them out). When you're by yourself for the vast majority of the day, you'll take whatever company you can get, even if they have horns and a beard (just as long as they're not chasing you).

My day of nature and solitude was interrupted (a rather welcome interruption) when I reached Blackstone. Not to say Blackstone was teeming with life, but there was a main street with shops and restaurants and a few people strolling about. It was nice to see a little activity and some smiling faces (of the human kind).

As I ran down Main Street, I passed the Wedgewood Motor Inn where I'm staying for the night. Had my hamstring been bothering me, I could have just called it a day and retired to my room. It would have made things easy and saved my parents the trouble of coming to get me. But all things considered, I was feeling pretty good, so I decided to press on and get all my miles in.

The problem was (there's always a problem, isn't there?) on the final approach to my ending point, I had to climb one of the biggest hills I've faced thus far. The ascent aggravated my hamstring, leaving me in pain. Adding to my troubles, Google Maps (or maybe the

Running The Coast For A Cure

person who entered the address into Google Maps) messed up because when I arrived at my "ending point" there was no church there as I was told there would be. Regardless of what (or who) was responsible, I soon learned that the actual location of the church, the true ending point, was another half mile up the road. This wouldn't have been a big deal, but, after running 22+ miles with a strained hamstring, 10 extra feet is burdensome. And of course, that extra half mile had me climbing another big hill.

By the time I reached the church, my hamstring was in considerable pain and I was exhausted. Fortunately for me, my parents had me back at the motel and off my feet in short order.

After showering and resting a bit, we headed out for dinner. My dad was excited to try this place he had scouted out earlier. It was a local restaurant with great food (or so he'd been told). Well, whoever told him that must have been delusional. The food was absolutely terrible. I only ate half my meal, and my mom barely touched hers. My dad ended up eating most of his, but I bet that was only because he picked the restaurant and didn't want to admit he'd made a bad choice. We left that place disappointed and (Mom and I) hungry.

Our next stop was a well-known establishment that was one of my go-to spots during my bike ride – Pizza Hut. After my two dinners (a turkey "surprise" and a cheese pizza with grilled chicken), I retired to my room with a full belly, a big bag of ice for my ailing hamstring, and a father-knows-best story to share with my siblings

Day 52 (10/29/14): Blackstone, VA to South Hill, VA [23.7 miles]

Since I strained my hamstring, I've been doing everything I can to nurse it back to health. Although there's no cure-all (trust me, there isn't; I've asked multiple experts, multiple times), the best remedy is rest. Unfortunately, there's only so much rest you can get when you're running just shy of a marathon each day.

I suppose I could take a day off and give it a real chance to heal, but with my parents being here I decided to keep plugging away. It's not often I have the logistics taken care of. And, if I encounter any problems during the day, I can always have them come get me.

There was yet another reason to press on. If my calculations were correct, after today's run, I'll be at 966 miles. According to Google Maps, as long as I don't have to take any detours or make any costly wrong turns, I'll have approximately the same number of miles to run as I've already covered before I reach Key Largo. That means the total number of miles for the entire run will end up being less than I originally thought, which I'm *definitely* not complaining about. It also means that after today's run, I'll be at the half-way point.

When I started today's run, I was surprised to find that my hamstring wasn't bothering me. It made me hopeful that yesterday's late-day pain was just a minor setback. It also had me thinking that as long as there weren't any big climbs today, I'd be okay.

The early part of the run took me past crop and animal farms and woodland of vibrant autumn colors. The road had few cars, which was good since there were long, shoulder-less stretches with little room to maneuver. The few drivers who did pass were much friendlier than those I'd encountered in previous days. Most gave me a wide berth, and many gave me a nod of the head or a thumbs-up. It was a welcome change from the "Southern In-hospitality" I'd experienced before.

About an hour and a half into it, I came to Kenbridge. Although I was in and out of town quickly, I did receive more friendly greetings, as well as some curious stares. I can't knock anyone for that. I'm sure the very sight of a stranger running through these close-knit communities raises questions. I figure as long as they're not running me off the road with their pickup trucks, it's all good.

Later in the day, the pain in my right hamstring flared up and forced me to slow my pace. It was both troubling and disappointing because I'd gone the better part of the day without any problems. Making matters worse, I didn't have the energy I normally do. I'm not sure if it was a result of the increased mileage (I'd been upping my miles as of late) or the hamstring injury, but either way I was completely worn-out.

The remainder of the run was grueling. My hamstring pain and fatigue had me plodding the flats and walking the inclines. Of course, that was when I wasn't standing

Running The Coast For A Cure

on the side of the road with my hands on my knees cursing and complaining. Yet, over the course of the last mile, the pain subsided (why or how I haven't a clue), allowing me to finish at a respectable pace.

The difficulties of the day soon turned to laughter when I approached the ending point (Shiloh Methodist Church) and realized my parents were confused as to which direction I'd be coming from. My mom was all set up to take photos of me but facing the *wrong* way. And my poor father had gone down the road about a quarter of a mile in the *wrong* direction and was waiting there in hopes of running to the finish with me. And this didn't just happen today; they've done things like this every day they've been with me. Talk about "directionally challenged." Luckily, my mom saw me before I got to the ending point and waved my dad back. She then repositioned herself (the right way this time) to capture the moment. After teasing them about it, I went down the road a ways with my dad, and we ran to the ending point together. The whole silly ordeal brought smiles to our faces and gave me another funny story to share.

Before leaving, my father pointed out the saying posted on the church's marquee: "The purpose of life is not to be happy: it is to make a difference." For me and my family, in the midst of this charity event, those words resonated. Yet, there is something more, something I didn't expect. Through my efforts, I have come to realize that when you strive to make a difference in the lives of others, you in turn find happiness.

Day 53 (10/30/14): South Hill, VA to Clarksville, VA [25.4 miles]

Yesterday I hit a milestone, the significance of which cannot be overstated. I'm now half-way to my final destination of Key Largo. Almost there! Well, not quite. Actually, not even close. There's still a *long* way to go and a lot of hard work ahead of me. But reaching the half-way point has me feeling optimistic. Also helping my outlook was that my hamstring felt much better today. For the first time in days, it felt strong, and I was able to run unrestricted.

My runs as of late have taken me past lots of farms. Today's run was no exception. The majority of them were crop farms, but there were a few animal farms sprinkled in. At one point, I ran past a half dozen cows that lifted their heads and turned toward me in unison. It was odd yet hilarious how they all fixated on me at the same time. I had to stop and take a picture, though when I did, I noticed one of the "cows" had sharp horns atop its head and an angry look in its eyes. I also realized nothing stood between us other than a few strings of barb-wire, so I thought it best to move along.

A little later, as I ran down a remote stretch of road I came to a point where another road dead-ended into the one I was on. Since the Google Maps' navigation lady

Al DeCesaris

(you know, that robotic feminine voice whispering in my ear) didn't say I needed to turn, I stayed on the road I was on. However, something didn't feel right. I checked Google Maps to make sure I was still going the right way. Well, sure enough, I did need to make that turn. I don't know what caused the problem, but had I not checked I would have ended up going miles out of my way. Moving forward, I'll have to keep a close eye on that navigation lady. She's not to be trusted.

About an hour later, I had another navigation scare, this one far worse. Out of nowhere, the road I was on turned into a narrow gravel road running between derelict old houses that looked like they were straight out of a horror movie. My first thought was that sly navigation lady has done it again and I'd have to backtrack. And when I was confronted by an unchained, enraged dog, I thought, backtrack or not, I need to get the heck out of here. Just before things escalated, a lady came out of her house and called off the dog. She then assured me the gravel road would get me to Clarksville (the day's ending point). It was a win-win *win* scenario – I didn't mace the dog, the dog didn't bite me, and I didn't have to backtrack.

Even so, it wasn't exactly a hop, skip, and jump back to civilization (you know you've lowered expectations when paved roads are the main criteria for civilization). I was on that gravel road in deserted rural land (with spotty cell phone service) for quite some time. After what seemed like an eternity, I reached Route 58. With

Running The Coast For A Cure

multiple lanes, a steady flow of traffic, and best of all, pavement, I felt like I was back in the land of the living.

That afternoon, I came to a bridge that took me over the John H. Kerr Reservoir. The sight of those billowy white clouds reflecting off the still blue waters was a sight to behold. It also helped make my time in that unsettling gravel-road-wasteland little more than an inconsequential footnote.

Just before 6pm, I crossed the Roanoke River and entered Clarksville. As I made my way through town, my big toe on my right foot started throbbing like someone had hit it with a sledgehammer. Although I was careful not to linger (I knew if I did my muscles would tighten up), I stopped, took off my shoe, and rubbed my toe to try to ease the pain. I can't say it worked 100%, but it was enough to get me back on my feet.

Once I got going, some random guy told me to pick up my feet when I run. *If I had the energy I would,* I thought. Yet, what I wanted to know was what Mr. Know-it-all's form would look like after running just shy of 1,000 miles.

I thought the ending point was just on the far side of Clarksville, though I soon realized it wasn't. At every corner I turned, I expected to see my parents there awaiting my arrival (and facing the wrong way), but there was no sign of them, and the road just continued on. I'm not sure if it was that navigation lady acting up again or operator error on my part, but the final stretch (which turned into several extra miles) seemed never-ending.

Al DeCesaris

After I was thoroughly exhausted, I caught sight of my parents standing out front of the ending point, Bobcat's Live Bait and Tackle. I don't know what was more surprising, the fact that there was actually a place called Bobcat's Live Bait and Tackle or that my parents were facing the right way for once.

Day 54 (10/31/14): Clarksville, VA to Oxford, NC [25.6 miles]

A few weeks back, I promised Elizabeth Medlock and her daughter Lily that I'd dress up on Halloween and parade around (rather, *run* around) in a costume. Lily is a huge superhero fan and if she had her way, I'd be wearing a superhero costume every day of my run. Well, today is October 31st (the *one day* I agreed to dress up), so I put on a Superman shirt and set out to do my best "Man of Steel" impersonation.

You're probably wondering what I'm doing with a Superman shirt. Long story short, Anna O'Herren got it for me. I'm not sure if Anna meant it as a joke, but I sure had a good laugh when I first saw it. Still, having it on hand for Halloween worked out perfectly.

Too bad my Superman costume didn't come with his superhuman powers. I could have used them today because for the second day in a row I'd be running over 25 miles. It wouldn't be easy, but I had something working in my favor. After 10 mentally and physically taxing days, I'd be leaving Virginia and entering "The Tar Heel State" of North Carolina. As you know, crossing state lines always gets me fired up.

After checking out of the hotel, we drove back to Bobcat's Live Bait and Tackle (that name still makes me

Al DeCesaris

laugh). Unfortunately, my parents had to head home today. The plan was for them to drive my car to the day's ending point in Oxford, North Carolina so it would be there when I finished the day's run. I'd then drive to the home of my childhood friend Brad Carpico where I'm staying for the next few days.

Although I was sad to see my parents go, I was thankful for our time together. Their support throughout the run has been amazing. And sharing this experience with them has meant the world to me.

After we said our goodbyes, I headed south down Route 15. I was happy to discover that yesterday's toe pain was barely noticeable, and my hamstring was no longer a concern. Even the cloudy sky and chilly temperatures weren't a problem for me. It must be the Superman shirt.

The early part of the run took me over a branch of the Roanoke River. It seems the Roanoke River and the John H. Kerr Reservoir, both of which I ran past yesterday, are one in the same. In fact, almost all of the water in the area is connected one way or the other to the river, or reservoir, or whatever the heck it's called.

About 12:30pm, I reached the state line. On one side of the road was a sign that read, "North Carolina state line" and on the other (facing the opposite direction) was one that read, "Virginia Welcomes You." Before the celebrating began, I jumped in front of the Virginia sign and snapped a selfie. If you recall, I didn't get a picture when I entered the state, so I needed to make sure I got one before I left. Anyway, one selfie soon turned into a

Running The Coast For A Cure

dozen because my noggin kept blocking the images of the flower and the bird on the sign (I figured if they're on the sign, they must be important). After a quick internet search, I discovered that Virginia's state flower is the American Dogwood and the state bird is the Cardinal. There you go, your daily dose of useless knowledge.

I then positioned myself in front of the North Carolina sign. This time I made sure my Superman shirt was visible in the picture. How could I not? I had just entered the state with the famous slogan, "First in Flight." Granted, it pays homage to Orville and Wilbur Wright, the America brothers who invented and built the world's first airplane, not the Kryptonian superhero who can fly "faster than a speeding bullet." Whatever, close enough.

Later, I came to an area that had tracks of packed dirt running along the road. As I've mentioned before, pavement can be hard on your feet and legs, so whenever I get the chance to run on softer ground, I take advantage of it. However, that isn't always the best course of action. Not far into it, I caught my foot on something and almost tumbled to the ground. Maybe I didn't have speeding cars to worry about, but rocks, holes, and twigs all over the place created their own share of problems. Unless I wanted to end up doing at a face-plant, I had to make sure I watched where I was running.

Toward the end of the run, I had another irritating navigation problem. After running what I thought was my 25.6 miles, the navigation lady said I had reached my destination. However, my car was nowhere to be seen

205

(it's now clear this "woman" has it out for me). My first thought was, it must be a glitch and that the destination was just a little farther ahead. But when I crested the next hill, I saw nothing but farmland.

I called Ida to see if she could figure out what was going on. After some time, she determined that I still had several miles to go. Hearing this got my blood boiling. *So, after running close to a marathon, I now have to run extra miles? Did I actually even run 25.6 miles? Did I have a wrong address entered in Google Maps all along?* I had no idea what had happened. And if Ida did, she wasn't sharing. The bottom line was, I still had several more miles to go and the sun was going down. At that point, I should have stepped it up, but I was dead-tired and over it, so I just walked the rest of the way. When I finally caught sight of the country market and spotted my car in their parking lot, it was a huge relief.

I then headed to Brad's house and got to his neighborhood just in time to get caught in a trick-or-treat traffic jam. After navigating through throngs of costumed kiddos, I reached the house and met Brad, his wife Julia, and their sons Nick and Christian (who were in their glory inventorying and inhaling Halloween candy). Under normal circumstances, I would have confiscated the Reese's Peanut Butter Cups and maybe the Sugar Babies too. But these are more health-conscious times. So instead, I ate several helpings of dinner and guzzled a bunch of sugar-filled energy drinks.

Day 55 (11/1/14): Oxford, NC to Durham, NC [21.9 miles]

The day started with a trip to Duke University Medical Center in Durham to meet Douglas Marchuk, Ph.D., Director of Molecular Genetics and Microbiology at the medical school. I had never met Dr. Marchuk, but I knew of him through his groundbreaking research of Sturge-Weber syndrome and was anxious to meet him.

Dr. Marchuk, along with Anne Comi, M.D. and Johnathan Pevsner, Ph.D., is one of the senior authors of the clinical research that produced the discovery of the genetic cause of Sturge-Weber syndrome. According to their research, published on May 8, 2013 in the *New England Journal of Medicine*, Sturge-Weber syndrome and port-wine birthmarks are caused by a somatic activating mutation in the *GNAQ* gene. The discovery is a game-changer and has given those living with Sturge-Weber syndrome real hope.

When Brad, Julia, Christian, and I (Nick couldn't join us) arrived, Dr. Marchuk greeted us warmly. I could tell he was excited to meet the relative of a child benefiting from his research. He gave us a tour of the hospital, medicine pavilion, and clinic. Duke University Medical Center was established in the 1920s by industrialist and philanthropist, James Buchanan Duke. Today, it is one

Al DeCesaris

of the preeminent medical centers in the country and its medical school consistently ranks in the top ten. The original School of Medicine building (now known as the Davison Building) was the highlight of the tour. It was designed in Collegiate Gothic-style reminiscent of a castle with two central towers on opposite sides of arched double doors. Above the entranceway were transom windows, ornate designs, and the shields of the renowned institutions Duke chose to model itself after.

We toured Dr. Marchuk's lab, and he told us about the work he and his team did that led to discovering the cause of Sturge-Weber syndrome. It was interesting to learn more about his role in the discovery and to learn how the discovery gives future research a direction and focus it never had before. This information also shines light on treatments and approaches to prevention previously unexplored.

As we made our way to the country market in Oxford where I left off, I couldn't help but think how exciting the possibilities were for my niece and all those living with Sturge-Weber syndrome. Imagine a world where Jenna and others like her – and their loved ones – don't have to live in constant fear of debilitating seizures and strokes ... of compromised or lost eyesight ... of contemptuous stares and ridicule. The potential of better treatments and one day, even a cure reinforced the importance of why I'm running to raise awareness and funds for Sturge-Weber syndrome research.

When we got to the market, it was cold and gloomy. On most days, this would have been a real downer. But

Running The Coast For A Cure

today, it didn't matter. I had a renewed sense of purpose. Plus, I had a running partner for the day (actually, for the next couple). Brad's a seasoned runner and knew how much it would help to have someone run with me, so he volunteered his time (and his legs).

The run started as yesterday's finished, on a narrow road with a narrow shoulder in a sea of farmland. Not far into it I turned my left ankle. When things like this happen (and they often do), I tend to tell myself that it was just one bad step (as though one bad step can't *possibly* cause an injury). Well this one "bad step" put a lot of pressure on my left shin and caused a lot of pain.

Not long after, it started drizzling and the temperature dropped. Brad and I weren't dressed for the rain or the cold for that matter. Yet, between funny old stories from our youth and new ones of my adventures on the road, we didn't let it bother us.

Later in the day, however, my right hamstring and right calf began to bother me. I'm not sure what caused the problems. It wasn't just one "bad step," that I can tell you. Whatever the culprit was, my hammy and calf got worse as the day wore on, as did my left shin. I've suffered many different aches, pains, and injuries, but it's rare for multiple ones to strike at the same time. I hoped this wasn't a precursor of things to come.

Around mile 20, we realized we weren't going to make it to our destination before the sun went down. So rather than risk running in the dark, we decided to call it a day and Julia picked us up. With my shin, hamstring, and calf issues, it was probably for the best anyway.

Al DeCesaris

Despite my smorgasbord of ailments and our shortened day, Brad and I managed to cover 21.9 miles. Even more noteworthy, we met Dr. Marchuk and learned how the groundbreaking discovery of the genetic cause of Sturge-Weber syndrome may very well lead to effective treatments, approaches to prevention, and possibly even a cure. If that doesn't keep me motivated to continue putting in miles, I don't know what will.

Day 56 (11/2/14): Durham, NC to Pittsboro, NC [26.5 miles]

According to the Encyclopedia Britannica, a marathon "commemorates the legendary feat of a Greek soldier who, in 490 BC, is supposed to have run from Marathon to Athens, a distance of about 40 km (25 miles), to bring news of the Athenian victory over the Persians ...." The marathon distance was later (some 2,400 years later) standardized to the 26 miles and 385 yards (first run at the 1908 Olympic Games in London) we know today. Since my charity run began almost two months ago, I've run 25 miles on three separate occasions, but haven't reached that elusive 26.2-mile mark (in fact, I had *never* run a marathon) ... until today.

For those who have run a marathon, you know, it's no easy feat. Actually, that's a gross understatement. A marathon is one of the hardest physical challenges an amateur athlete can take on. Still, in light of what I've accomplished thus far (running more than 1,000 miles), I felt confident I could do it. I also had Brad running with me again to keep me company and help push me along. We also had a top-notch cheering section in Julia, Nick, and Christian, who were going to meet us at various points with drinks and snacks as we made our way to our destination in Pittsboro.

Al DeCesaris

Brad and I started our run at the VFW Post where we left off yesterday and soon made our way into downtown Durham. The city experienced tremendous growth during the heyday of the tobacco industry, and in recent years has seen significant revitalization. Our route took us past a number of redevelopment projects, the new Durham Bulls Athletic Park, the Durham Performing Arts Center as well as some old tobacco factories that have been converted into multi-use projects with residences, shops, restaurants, and office space.

After leaving downtown Durham, we found ourselves climbing into Chapel Hill. The town takes its name from the hill it sits atop, which was once home to an Anglican chapel built in the 1750s. In addition to its southern charm and beauty (it doesn't have the motto "The Southern Part of Heaven" for nothing), Chapel Hill is the quintessential college town for the nation's first public university, the University of North Carolina.

Brad and I met Julia and the boys on campus. After a short break and a few photos together, Nick and Christian ran with us for a little while. (Oh, if only I had their energy.) We then made our way over to the Old Well. Although I'd never heard of it, I soon learned that the Old Well (circa 1897) is the university's most enduring landmark. According to tradition, if a student drinks from the Old Well on the first day of classes, they will get straight As. I can only imagine how long the line must be to get up to that thing on the first day of each new school year. Too bad we didn't have an Old Well at my alma mater … I might have graduated on time.

Running The Coast For A Cure

Julia and the boys then headed back to the car as Brad and I picked up the pace in hopes of reaching our destination (and covering our marathon miles) before nightfall. Even before we saw what we were up against we knew it was going to be tough. We had started late and stopped several times throughout the day, leaving us short on time. We pushed hard and covered the first several hilly miles quickly. However, what I thought was just a couple of isolated hills was actually a series of them, one bigger than the next. Despite our best efforts, our pace and our energy waned, as did the sunlight. With about two miles to go, Julia and the boys met us to see how we were doing. We could have called it a day with a respectable 24-mile run to our credit, but Brad and I wanted to finish what we had set out to do. We wanted to complete the marathon. So, we continued on.

Those last couple of miles seemed to take forever, but when we caught sight of Julia and the kids waving and cheering in front of our destination (Allen & Son Bar-B-Que) the pain and fatigue of the 26.5-mile run melted away. We celebrated the achievement with hi-fives, hugs, and the victory drink of choice, Gatorade. Both Brad and Julia had run a marathon before, but this was my first. Although I'm sure it's great to do it in the company of other runners, with crowds cheering you on, I was thrilled to have run my first marathon with my old friend and with the support and encouragement of his loving family. In fact, I couldn't think of a better way to mark our time together.

Day 57 (11/3/14): Pittsboro, NC to Sanford, NC [26.6 miles]

From the moment I got started, I knew it was going to be a tough day. I'm sure most people take time off after running a marathon to recover. Even if they don't, I doubt they run another marathon the following day. Well, as crazy as that sounds, that was the plan my *sweet* and *loving* sister had made for me. It's pretty obvious Ida has become quite the taskmaster. All kidding (and complaining) aside, I knew that during the second half of the run I'd have to increase my daily average mileage. Otherwise, I'd be on the road into late December or worse. So, there I was running my second marathon (26.6 miles to be exact) in as many days.

Unfortunately, Brad had to work, so I was going it alone. However, he did say that if he wrapped things up early, he'd come meet me and run the last few miles with me. I hoped that would be the case because having his company has been a big help. Plus, conversations with imaginary friends get a little weird after a while.

Within a few miles, Route 15/Route 501 (the two highways run concurrently and are often referred to as 15-501) crossed over the Haw River. From the bridge I had an amazing view of the water as it flowed between large rocks and around shrub-covered islets scattered throughout the river. One islet even had several big trees with leaves displaying a palette of autumn colors.

About an hour later, I reached downtown Pittsboro. The quaint little historic town had one main road with numerous restaurants, cafes, shops, and art galleries. Its main attraction (in this lawyer's opinion) is the Chatham County Courthouse, which sits in the middle of a traffic circle in the heart of town. Built in the 1880s, it's a Late-Victorian style building with a portico and a central clock tower. In 2010, it suffered extensive fire damage and had to be restored. I don't know what it looked like before, but I'd say they restored it to its former glory and then some.

Little did I know that running through Pittsboro would be the highlight of my day. Just beyond the downtown area, I came to a great expanse of woodland. There, 15-501 widened, straightened, and leveled out, revealing indistinguishable landscape as far as the eye could see. The monotony of it went on and on.

The worse part of it all was not having any music. That's right, at some point along that mind-numbing stretch of road, my earbuds died. Now, I realize it's *possible* to run without music, and apparently there are people who can actually do it. But, for me, running without music is cruel and unusual punishment.

Later, 15-501 intersected with Route 1. Yep, the same Route 1 I've run on time and again. Even though it would have been good to get back on it (it's a more direct route and would have been a welcome change of scenery), this section of Route 1 prohibits pedestrians.

Running The Coast For A Cure

So, I was stuck on 15-501 and forced to go through downtown Sanford.

A bit later, I got the call from Brad. He had worked things out and was able to join me. It was awesome news. I was dragging and could really use his help getting my miles in and closing out the day.

My run through downtown Sanford was a blur. Not because I ran through it so fast, that *definitely* wasn't the case. It was a blur because I was exhausted and on the phone with Brad the whole time trying to figure out where we were going to meet. It's tricky coordinating a meeting point when you're in an unfamiliar area and on foot.

We eventually did connect, but not until I reached the far side of the city. The timing though, worked out just fine. We started our run together on a narrow, winding road with a tiny shoulder. Minutes in, it became a high-stress dash among speeding cars. Having Brad there to lead the way and set the pace was a godsend. With his help and encouragement, I was able to navigate those dangerous roads and fight through my fatigue.

Just before the end of the run, Google Maps directed us onto Route 1 (this section allows pedestrians). Brad and I trotted the last half mile to the ending point, Hardee's, as the sun went down. Like yesterday, Julia and the kids were there to congratulate us. Also, like yesterday, I had completed a marathon distance. To think, a few days ago I had never run a marathon. Now I have back-to-back marathons under my belt.

217

Day 58 (11/4/14): Sanford, NC to Aberdeen, NC [26.6 miles]

After breakfast, I packed my things and said my goodbyes to the Carpicos. My time with them has been one of the highlights of the run. Before parting ways, Brad helped me get my car situated at the day's ending point in Aberdeen. He then dropped me off in Sanford where we left off. Brad's kindness and generosity (and leg-power) were a tremendous help. I'll be forever grateful for everything he has done for me.

As soon as I started the day's run, I could tell it was going to be a real struggle. There was no denying it. I was *completely* wiped out. I guess back-to-back marathons will do that to you. Even so, the plan was to run yet another one (another 26.6 miles). How I was going to manage that? I hadn't a clue.

The only thing working in my favor was I had music again. Will Futch had left a pair of earbuds for me at his condo in D.C. I didn't think I'd need them, but I brought them with me just in case. Boy am I glad I did. I could barely survive running one day without music. Things would have gotten ugly had I been forced to go another.

I followed Route 1 through numerous commercial areas. Being back on the highway, I figured I wouldn't see much rural land for some time (which was fine with

Al DeCesaris

me). However, that wasn't the case. About two hours in, Google Maps had me exit off of Route 1 onto Route 1 Business. Now you'd think a road with "Business" in its name would be in an area with, I don't know, *businesses*. Apparently, that isn't how it works. This particular road led me back into country-fried rural land.

A half hour later, I got held up at a fowl crossing. Seriously, a couple dozen birds were parading across the road, one after the other. Lord knows why, but I stood there patiently waiting for the procession to end. If that wasn't strange enough, they were marching toward a sign on the side of the road that read, "FRESH EGGS $2.50." So, am I to assume these ladies were headed to work? If so, did they get paid by the egg or the hour? Sorry, I couldn't resist.

Just before 2pm, I passed two buildings painted with a panoramic mural of a farm with cows, pigs, horses, and other animals. I admit, it was well done and even got me to stop and take a picture. But come on, wasn't there enough farm life around these parts to look at? Did they really need a farm mural in the heart of farm land?

Soon after, some hillbilly (and that's putting it nicely) steered his pickup truck over the outside white line and onto the shoulder I was running in. *What the heck is this guy doing?* I asked as the truck raced toward me. Whatever he was up to, it wasn't good. Panic-stricken, I leaped out of the way. He sneered at me as if to say, "I got you," before pulling back into his lane and flying by. Well, he did indeed "get me", and I got a new candidate for the biggest S.O.B. of the run award.

Running The Coast For A Cure

I then returned to Route 1, though it wasn't the smooth sailing I hoped for. The shoulder along this stretch was very small, and the road was seething with tractor trailers. My visor flew off my head at least a half dozen times from the wind created by the speeding rigs. It was funny at first, but then having to run after it every five minutes like a dog fetching a stick got *very* irritating.

As I continued along, the shoulder got even smaller while the number of vehicles and their increased speed. As though things weren't nerve-wracking enough, a rumble strip ran down the middle of the shoulder. It was uncomfortable to run on and had me concerned I'd turn an ankle or injury my feet. After a few minutes, I decided it wasn't worth the risk and started walking in the grass alongside the roadway.

Walking those miles made for a very long day. It would have been even longer had I not caught a break when I reached Southern Pines. On the approach into town the road is bordered by, you guessed it, pine trees, but in town it's bordered by sidewalks. After hours of slow-going frustration, I was able to run again, safe from speeding vehicles. I was also fortunate that the sidewalk continued into neighboring Aberdeen and to my car.

It was a super-long day (both mileage and time-wise) and it sure wasn't pretty. But, when it was all said and done, I had a third consecutive marathon to my credit. It's a testament to what we (all of us) can achieve when we put our minds and hearts to something we believe in.

Day 59 (11/5/14): Aberdeen, NC to Laurinburg, NC [21.1 miles]

In the morning I drove to the day's ending point, a church on the outskirts of Laurinburg. Actually, the term "outskirts" doesn't paint an accurate picture. It may have had a Laurinburg address, but this place was in no man's land, miles from Laurinburg proper. Since I would have to suffer through yet another "rural run," I hoped this one wouldn't include any hillbillies in pickup trucks.

After getting the church's "blessing" (pun *most definitely* intended) to leave my car in their parking lot, I got a ride back to yesterday's ending point from Jennifer from Walgreens. It had been a while since we needed Anna O'Herren's help. But when we put in the call, Anna and Walgreens came through for us yet again.

It was about 9:30am when I started my run. Mentally I felt good, though physically I felt like I was falling apart. The three consecutive marathons had taken their toll on me (that and running 13 days straight). This became evident last night as I laid awake in bed, tossing and turning with aches and pains in my right and left calves, right and left hamstrings, right quadriceps, right upper back, and right shoulder. I suppose it would have been easier to list the parts of my body that weren't hurting. Needless to say, a day of rest is *long* overdue.

Al DeCesaris

A few minutes into the run, Google Maps' walking route had me turn off of Route 1 back onto 15-501. I'd just driven this stretch of road (as I made my way to the church and back) so I knew what it held – hilly woodland dominated by pine trees. Not the most exciting stuff, though there was something of interest in this area. Visible in certain places were tell-tale signs of the Sandhills – ancient beach dunes situated in the interior of the Carolinas, believed to be the former coastline that existed back in the day (like 20 million years back in the day). I had noticed the unique landscape yesterday as I approached Southern Pines, but I was too busy chasing my visor to give it much consideration. Today, however, I had plenty of time to take it in. The ground had the color and texture of sand on a beach. It was wild to see the creams and tans of this unique soil contrasted against the greens and coppers of the pine needles on the trees and those on the ground.

Like the stretch of Route 1 I was on toward the latter part of yesterday's run, 15-501 had a small shoulder with a rumble strip running down the middle of it. For the second day in a row, I was forced into the grass alongside the road. It was annoying, though it fit into my plan for the day.

Taking into consideration the number of miles I'd covered recently and how my body felt, the plan was not to push myself too hard. That's code for cover fewer miles at a super slow pace (i.e. walking). However, there were a couple of problems with that. First, I *have to* maintain a certain number of miles per day, even on a

224

Running The Coast For A Cure

day like this when I'm struggling. The other problem was that walking is boring, excruciatingly so.

I stuck to the plan as best I could (rather as long as my impatient-self allowed), but, as the day wore on, I started to run a little. To pull that off on this road, I had to step into the roadway when there was a break in traffic and cover as much ground as I could before any cars got close. I was careful not to push things too far. I've had my fill of malevolent maniac drivers trying to run over me. I didn't need to spur any on.

When there was too much traffic, I tried my hand at running on the sliver of pavement between the rumble strip and grass. It couldn't have been more than three or four inches wide and seemed to get even smaller when cars came flying by. There were a few missteps at first, but after a while I got the hang of it, more or less. Between the two techniques, I managed to get some running in ... or something that resembled it.

As much as I dreaded running the rural back-roads, when I turned off 15-501 and got onto them, I was quite relieved. There might not have been anything exciting to see, but at least I was able to run unabated. Plus, it meant I was close to the day's ending point.

I reached my car around 3pm. Although I didn't make the fastest time, the day's "don't push it too hard" plan worked well. I finished without any problems and even managed to carve out some late afternoon recovery time. I was told to listen to my body. After three marathons the previous three days, the message was unmistakable – my body needed R&R in the worst way.

Day 61 (11/7/14): Laurinburg, NC to Bennettsville, SC [21 miles]

I could tell even before loosening up that my legs were feeling much better today. In fact, I was feeling great. A day of rest (or shall I say, a day of rain) will do that for you. It wasn't raining cats and dogs (or even kittens and puppies), though it was coming down steadily enough to convince me to take the day off.

I also felt great because today I'd be crossing into South Carolina. It'd be my 12th state (with only Georgia and Florida remaining). Granted, Florida is the largest state I'll run through, and it'll probably take me the better part of three weeks. And to get there, I'll have to suffer through South Carolina and Georgia for about two weeks. But who's counting weeks? I'm focused on states now; it's a much more manageable number.

After breakfast, I drove to the day's ending point, a convenience store in Bennettsville. There, I met Dustin, another Walgreens' employee who volunteered to help. Once the store manager convinced me my car would be safe in their parking lot (it didn't take a genius to realize this wasn't the safest area), Dustin gave me a ride to the church where I left off the day before last.

When I got started, the sky was blue and the sun was shining, giving even the desolate farmland a certain charm. I'd gotten a prevue of the area when we drove in, but I had no idea exactly what I'd see. Unless you drive the same roads you're running, you never really know.

One thing I didn't expect to see were cotton fields. I knew they were prevalent in the south, but up until then I hadn't come across any. At first glance, it appeared as though the fields had gotten a dusting of snow. Even after I got a better look, I thought, *snow*. It was hard to wrap my brain around fields with cotton growing in them. Before that, the only thing I knew for certain was cotton was the material my t-shirts were made of.

Not long after, my right quadriceps started to bother me. It was just subtle discomfort at first, but it caught me off guard. I had just taken a day off. Why would I be having problems? My surprise turned into concern the moment the discomfort turned into pain.

As you know, when things like this happen, I implement my "maintenance check." However, even after going through it (and walking for a while) the pain persisted. Worse yet, the pain intensified and radiated from just above my knee up to my hip. I wasn't taking any chances with it, so I shut it down and put a call into John Wall to find out what I should do … or not do.

As I walked and awaited John's return call, three mangy mutts charged across an open field toward me. I wasn't sure what the deal was, but they did *not* look like they were coming to play. I had no chance of outrunning them, so I stopped and stood still. That's supposed to be one of the best ways to ward off attacking dogs. Well, it didn't work on these three. I then tried to shoo them away with loud forceful commands and exaggerated hand gestures, to no avail. One of the dogs started circling around me while the other two moved in from the front. That was enough for me. I pulled out my mace and sprayed it in the air. At first it seemed to work, but they soon went back on the offensive. In the end, it took about half a bottle of mace to get them to back off.

Minutes later, I spotted a sign that read, "South Carolina STATE LINE." Despite quad and canine issues, I was elated to reach "The Palmetto State." I moved into position and snapped my requisite selfies, though I had to be quick about it. Those mangy mutts were still visible in the distance, and if I could see them, they could see me ... plus, I was running low on mace.

I then spoke to John Wall and his wife Michel. They love Jenna and have been super supportive of my efforts to fight Sturge-Weber syndrome on her behalf. John even rode with me the first day of my bike ride for which I will always be thankful. After catching up, I told John about my quad problem. He wasn't as concerned about it as I thought he'd be. He told me as long as I'm careful with it, I should be able to run on it without causing further damage. That was such a relief to hear.

The positive news gave me the confidence I needed to finish the day's run at a respectable pace. I reached Bennettsville around 4:30pm and arrived at the convenience store and my car (which was still there as promised), soon after. It wasn't my fastest day, but all things considered, I was lucky to make it through it in one piece ... and without getting rabies.

Day 62 (11/8/14): Bennettsville, SC to Darlington, SC [24.5 miles]

After my morning meal and going over my pre-run checklist, I drove to the day's ending point, a church on Route 52 in Darlington, where I met Tyler from Walgreens. After securing my car key in my hydration pack, I hopped into Tyler's car and he gave me a ride to the convenience store in Bennettsville where I left off. Credit Anna O'Herren with yet another ride. For those keeping track, that's the sixth one she's arranged.

The plan was to follow Route 15 to the town of Society Hill, then take Route 52 to Darlington. Ida picked that particular church as the ending point because it was located right along my route, a distance from the starting point she felt I could handle … and because she was able to get permission for me to leave my car there (don't underestimate the impact that has on things). It was a great plan *in theory*; the problem was, the route was 24.5 miles and I was in pain even when walking.

Based on what John said yesterday, I figured I'd wake up feeling halfway decent. I now realize that was naïve. I had a quadriceps strain, and things like that don't heal overnight. So, the *new* plan was to protect my quad while still getting my miles in (all 24.5 of them). What that boiled down to was lots of walking and as little running as possible. I figured, if I had enough time, I'd walk the entire way. The way I looked at it, it was a rest day of sorts. Of course, I could have taken an actual rest day, but since I'd recently taken a day off, I decided against it. This was the in-between solution – I'd be giving my quad a break while still covering my miles.

When I started, it was cloudy, and temps were in the high 50s. As soon as I left Bennettsville proper, I found myself back in the lonesome countryside. First it was farms, then woodland. Even so, the scenery was nice. Some of the leaves had a smattering of fall colors while others held onto their vibrant greens in defiance of the change of seasons. At times I wondered if I had outrun autumn; I then realized (and not just because I was walking at a turtle-like pace) that I hadn't outrun anything. Autumn in the south is just different than it is up north. Still, it has its own unique beauty.

About 10 miles in, I crossed the Great Pee Dee River and entered Society Hill. Now, I didn't need to mention the name of the river, but I figured any body of water that has the word "Pee" in its name is worth mentioning. Sad to say, Society Hill didn't seem to have anything as exciting about it, at least at first glance. As I left town, a car rolled by with a gorgeous brunette behind the wheel. For a second, I thought she was checking me out. Then I realized she was gawking at me like I'd escaped an insane asylum. How could she not? I was sporting running apparel and a hydration pack on my back yet walking like an ailing old-timer. I didn't know whether to hide my head in shame or laugh. As I got onto Route 52

Running The Coast For A Cure

and left Society Hill (and the gorgeous brunette) behind, I did a bit of both.

After that humbling incident, you'd think I would throw caution to the wind, pick up the pace and run. My pride sure wanted me to. But I knew better. My quad was bothering me even while walking. The best course of action was to stick to the plan. The problem was I still had another 10 miles to go and daylight was slipping away. I again considered running, but I knew I needed to stay disciplined to protect my leg.

Those last 10 miles were challenging, physically because of my quad and mentally because walking for hours when you want to run is demoralizing. The last couple of miles, though, were the worst. The sun went down, and the road narrowed to such an extent that I was confined to a paltry strip of grass right next to the road's outside white line. I hoped and prayed drivers could see me. Well, this one guy (who I *know* saw me) jerked the wheel towards me just as he passed, coming alarmingly close. Minutes later, a tractor-trailer blasted his horn as he barreled by. The two incidents left me angry and disheartened … and wondering if they would have done those things had they known I was doing this for charity and that I was battling a leg injury.

As I closed out the day, my thoughts shifted from their inexplicable actions to my own. *What am I doing out here?* I questioned, even though I knew better. I was letting my emotions get the best of me. Still, the self-doubt and feelings of loneliness were overwhelming. It was a very frustrating end to a very difficult day.

Day 63 (11/9/14): Darlington, SC to Bishopville, SC [24.4 miles]

In the morning, I drove to the day's ending point, a country market on Route 401 in Bishopville. There, I met Jerry from … you guessed it, Walgreens. Jerry had agreed to give me a ride and even offered to do it tomorrow and the next day. It's very kind when someone volunteers their time to help one day, but to do it for three consecutive days is astounding.

After I got permission to leave my car at the market, Jerry drove me to the church in Darlington where I left off. Before I began, a man approached me and asked if I was the guy who parked in the church parking lot yesterday. My first thought was that I was going to get reprimanded (I *thought* Ida said she got permission, but I wasn't certain). After admitting that I was the one who parked there, he said he was from the church and that he had shared my story with his congregation. He wished me well and said they'd keep me in their prayers. What a relief and what a blessing. I could use all the prayers I could get.

As I started down Route 52 for the first of 24.4 miles, I thought how nice of him it was to do that. I also noted how much the kind words and actions of others affect the way you feel. I had a very bad day yesterday. Yet, after talking with this man, whom I had never seen before and would likely never see again, I had a positive outlook and was eager to take on the day.

I would, however, take on the day at a slow, careful pace. Like yesterday, the plan was to walk as much as possible. I'd had enough problems over the past couple of months; I didn't need another lingering injury. One more day of walking wouldn't be the end of the world.

Not far into it, I passed a guy who asked where I was headed. I'm always curious what kind of reaction I'll get when I tell people I'm headed to Florida. Well, his was priceless. He didn't respond with words at first, but the look on his face said it all. I think if a UFO with aliens had touched down at that very moment, it would have made more sense to him.

Later in the day, another guy rode by and asked me if I was okay. Although we only spoke briefly, I could tell his concern was genuine. My interactions today couldn't have been more different from yesterday's. If this was the new trend, I couldn't wait for my next interaction with a gorgeous brunette (or blond or redhead).

Around 3:30pm, I passed a cotton field. While those I saw outside of Laurinberg looked like they'd been dusted with snow, this one looked like it had several inches of fresh powder on it. Perhaps people who live near them aren't impressed, but I find them fascinating.

As I passed a house with a fenced-in yard, I caught sight of a menacing dog racing toward the fence and watched in horror as it somehow slipped under it. A split second later another dog ran out of the woods just down from the house. This one was big and nasty and looked like a stray. I wasn't taking any chances with these two; I stopped in my tracks and went right for the mace. Whether they sensed what I was doing or lost interest when I stopped, I wasn't sure, but they abandoned their pursuit. It was a huge relief, but the incident left me wondering what I had done to become "Public Enemy No. 1" of the canine community.

Despite my efforts to reach the day's ending point before nightfall, I found myself on the road after dark. Fortunately, my quad was holding up well (I had little more than subtle discomfort the entire day). And there was a wide grassy area alongside the roadway where I could safely walk.

As I covered the last mile, a guy on a farm tractor rolled by and asked if I needed a lift. No joke. This hospitable southerner offered me a ride. After respectfully and *regrettably* declining his offer (closing out the day on a tractor would have made a great "you know you're in the south when…" story), I continued on and soon reached the country market and my car.

You would think, as much as I've run over the past two months, walking would be easy for me. Well, that isn't the case. Maybe you use different muscles when you walk, or maybe you use your muscles in different ways. Whatever the reason, walking close to a marathon is hard and tedious work. Yet, like the motto of South Carolina – "Dum spiro spero," which is Latin for "While I breathe, I hope" – I'm still breathing, and I hope tomorrow brings a return to running.

Day 64 (11/10/14): Bishopville, SC to Sumter, SC [20.9 miles]

This morning I met Jerry at the day's ending point, a Food Lion in Sumter. He greeted me with a bag of energy bars, courtesy of him and his staff at the Walgreens he manages. It was very kind of them and greatly appreciated, especially since I go through several energy bars a day. Jerry then drove me to the country market in Bishopville where I left off yesterday.

After two straight days of walking, today I would return to running, which was cause for celebration. Even though my right quad felt good and the distance was a "mere" 21 miles, I knew I should take it easy. So, the plan was to run at a safe pace and take lots of breaks.

When I got started, the temperature was in the 60s and there was decent cloud cover, making for great running conditions. This stretch of Route 401, however, was narrow with no shoulder and there was little to see other than farmland. I was *so* looking forward to my time in South Carolina. I had visited Charleston some years back and assumed the entire state held that historic elegance, charm and beauty. Wow was I mistaken! The vast majority of what I've seen thus far is dull and desolate rural land. Thank goodness for those cotton

Al DeCesaris

fields and the occasional crazy canine. Otherwise, I might have died of boredom.

Speaking of cotton, a bit before noon I ran past monstrous cotton bails. There must have been close to 20 of them, each with a diameter of about six feet. After seeing cotton in the fields these past few days, it was interesting to see it after being picked … and ready to be shipped to the t-shirt factories of the world.

A little later, I ran past a man standing in front of his house who asked where I was headed. Like the guy yesterday, he was dumbfounded when he learned I was headed to Florida. This time, though, I made sure to emphasize that I had started in Maine just to see how high I could ratchet up his "disbelief meter." In these sleepy, remote areas I have to do what I can to keep myself entertained.

Later in the day, it started to get warmer. As I ran, the heat had me working up a sweat. It was a welcome change from walking with a dry brow for hours on end. It made me feel like I was really back at it. Then again, so did the random discomfort and pain, which I inevitably seem to have. Today, it was my right shoulder and the upper right part of my back, both of which had bothered me before. Also, as the day wore on, the arch of my right foot started hurting. Yep, I was definitely back at it.

Today, however, my pain and discomfort were not the concern. My thoughts were on Jenna as she was having surgery on her right eye to reduce the escalating intraocular pressure caused by Glaucoma. Through this procedure, Select Laser Trabeculoplasty, laser energy is applied to the eye's drainage tissue. When successful, this initiates a change in the tissue leading to better drainage of fluid and thus a reduction in the eye's intraocular pressure. The results of the procedure take several months to determine and, even when successful, don't permanently resolve the problem. Sad to say, at the present, there is no lasting treatment for this condition. Yet, if the pressure isn't regulated now and continuously maintained within safe levels, the limited vision she has will be at significant risk.

Eventually, the countryside gave way to the city of Sumter. Although there wasn't anything exciting to see, just being around activity was a good distraction from my worries. It was also good that the city had sidewalks where I could run, safe from speeding cars and trucks.

A couple of miles in, I turned onto Route 15 and followed it through the south side of Sumter. Unfortunately for me, through this area there were no sidewalks. Even worse, along this stretch, Route 15 turned into a major highway with two lanes going in each direction, no shoulder, and vehicles flying by at high speeds. It forced me to finish out the day in the grass alongside the roadway.

Still, on a day when Jenna's struggles were front and center, my minor inconveniences were of little consequence, as were my discomfort and pain. The challenges I've faced during this run, although at times quite difficult, are only temporary. In contrast, the adversity Jenna has to deal with is ever present. That is why I run. That is why we *must* find a cure.

Day 65 (11/11/14): Sumter, SC to Summerton, SC [19.8 miles]

Jerry picked me up this morning at the day's ending point, a motel in Summerton right on my route. I love it when my day starts or ends at a motel like that. It allows for a little less driving and a little more sleeping. That is, of course, if you're staying at the motel, which I most definitely wasn't. (If you had seen that skeevy, dilapidated place, you wouldn't have stayed there either.) Jerry then drove me back to the Food Lion in Sumter where I left off. It was our last day together, so I thanked him for all of his generous support.

Like yesterday, it was to be another short day, just shy of 20 miles. Mileage-wise this wasn't where I wanted to be (or needed to be). Yet, I was far from 100%. I figured it was best not to push my luck. It was a great day for a run, though. The sun was shining, and the temperature was in the low 70s.

Not long after starting, I passed some Southern live oaks with Spanish moss hanging from the branches. For me, Spanish moss is one of those things that screams "Deep South." Bless your heart, y'all know what I'm talkin 'bout.

As I was making my way down Route 15's narrow shoulder, a tractor-trailer came barreling by so fast –

Al DeCesaris

and so close – that it sent my visor flying through the air a good 15 feet. I didn't find this amusing like I did the last time this happened, not even a little. Having to stop and go back to retrieve it was downright annoying. Still, I knew it could have been worse. That could have been me (or my head) flying through the air.

As I ran down the road, the suburban area outside of Sumter gave way to undeveloped land. About that time, a chicken truck drove by. I know I've whined and moaned about this before, but that ungodly stench has to be one of the worse on the planet. It left me gagging and nauseous, and wondering how the heck I eat those foul fowl knowing what they smell like.

A bit later, I passed a gas station and saw and heard a girl cheering me on. Did she know I was doing a charity run? Or was she cheering for me because I was braving that narrow shoulder and all the speeding cars (and chicken trucks)? Whatever the case, it was cool to have the encouragement. I never get tired of that.

Route 15 then began to narrow and after a couple of miles became your typical country road with one lane going in each direction and no shoulder to speak of. Rather than plodding along in the grass, I decided to run on the road's outside white line. I know this isn't the safest thing to do, but the road was straight and flat, and I could see when cars were coming toward me. The plan, however, did have one major flaw. I couldn't see the lunatic driver in the pickup truck that was flying up behind me and had crossed the yellow line to pass another vehicle. When the truck passed me, it came so close that it almost plowed into me. I might not have seen it coming, but I definitely felt the gust of wind as the truck whizzed by.

Later in the day, I ran past a man fishing in a pond on the side of the road. He asked where I was headed. When I told him Summerton, he stared at me with a raised eyebrow and said, "boy, you got a *long* way to go." It had me laughing because at that point Summerton was only five more miles down the road. I could only imagine how he would have reacted if I had told him Florida.

Toward the end of the day's run, my right quadriceps started to bother me again. I wasn't sure if I'd aggravated it or if this was the result of a new injury. Either way, it left me frustrated and concerned. And that wasn't my only problem. I also had nagging pain on the right side of my back, which I'd been dealing with most of the day.

Out of nowhere another lunatic almost blind-sided me as he crossed the yellow line and passed multiple cars. *What the heck is going on!?!* I hadn't had to worry about this kind of thing before. Now, twice in one day, I nearly got struck from behind. I had no idea why, but Route 15 through these parts seemed like the "hillbilly autobahn."

Over the last few miles, the pain in my quad got worse, convincing me to shut it down. As I walked to my car, my frustration and concern was overtaken by anger. I was sick and tired of not being healthy, and sick and tired of these lunatic drivers and desolate roads. I need to get healthy, and I need to get out of this rural abyss.

Day 66 (11/12/14): Summerton, SC to Harleyville, SC [27.1 miles]

It was a crazy day from the start. When I woke up, I received a call from Ida informing me that what we thought was going to be a 25-mile day was actually going to be 27 miles. Apparently, there had been a miscalculation (either that or she was trying to kill me).

After relaying my concerns and reminding her that I'd been battling injuries the better part of the past week, Ida tried to find a closer ending point. The problem was, this part of South Carolina is mostly undeveloped, leaving me with limited options of where I could leave my car. The only other spot she could find was 15 miles from the starting point. That was way too short. I'd been in South Carolina long enough. I needed to get the heck out of here, so I decided to go with the 27-mile run.

After a bit of convincing (and a cash incentive), J.D., one of the innkeepers of the motel where I'm staying, followed me to the day's ending point, a gas station in Harleyville. I parked my car in the parking lot so it would be there when I finished my marathon plus mileage. J.D. then drove me to the motel in Summerton where I left off yesterday.

When I started the day's run, the sun was shining, and the temperature was in the mid 70s. There was a

Al DeCesaris

nice breeze as well, making for a gorgeous day. Also working to my benefit, this stretch of Route 15 was straight and flat with minimal traffic. It was a welcome change from yesterday's terrifyingly close-calls.

Around 11am, I saw a detour sign and noticed that the road ahead was blocked. *Detour?* I questioned. Google Maps had me following Route 15 to Lake Marion, then taking an old pedestrian-friendly bridge across the lake. The bridge was only another three and half miles ahead. There was no way I was taking a detour and adding miles, and potentially ending up on a road (or worse, a bridge) I wasn't allowed to be on.

The news of this had my family scouring the internet and calling local businesses to figure out if I could continue past this point and take the old bridge across the lake. If I couldn't, this would pose a *major* problem. The only other options were: taking I-95, which had a bridge that crossed the lake (although it prohibited pedestrians) or going around the lake. The latter wasn't a realistic option because I'd have to go about 30 miles out of my way. That *definitely* wasn't happening! Even though my family never received a definitive answer, the general consensus from the locals was, they "thought" I could stay on Route 15 and the old bridge "should" get me across the lake. It wasn't the most reassuring answer I've ever heard, but it was enough to convince me to continue on.

Just before noon, I came upon more barriers and a sign that read, "ROAD CLOSED." As I slipped between the barriers, I thought, *No turning back now.* The road

248

Running The Coast For A Cure

took me over Cantey Bay and smack into the middle of road construction. Lucky for me, the construction workers were on break. By the time they noticed me, I was on the far side of their heavy machinery. I soon realized, however, that this wasn't the problem area. Sure, there was construction, and the road was "technically" closed, but the real concern was getting over Lake Marion. *Is that old bridge open? It had better be!* I kept asking – and telling – myself as I ran onward.

About 15 minutes later, I came to another "ROAD CLOSED" sign, this one right in front of the old bridge. There didn't appear to be any construction up ahead, leading me to believe that the bridge was no longer in use. At that point, I could have backtracked to I-95 and taken my chances with the cars and cops on the pedestrian-restricted bridge. Still, my best (and safest) option was this old bridge. So, I again slipped between the barriers and made my way onto it.

The bridge appeared to be structurally sound, though I couldn't tell how far it went. I followed it about a quarter of a mile onto an islet in the lake. Sometimes with bridges that are no longer in use, rather than tear the whole thing down, parts of them are left intact for use as fishing piers. I sure hoped that wasn't the case here. I had to go another three quarters of a mile to the end of the islet before I could tell for certain. From that point, I could see that the bridge remained intact and extended the entire way over Lake Marion to the town of Santee. It was a huge relief. After all that fuss and worry, running across the old bridge was like taking a victory lap.

249

South of Santee, Route 15 turned back into a rural tree-lined road with a narrow shoulder and a rumble strip running through the outside white line, leaving me little room to run. And the old woman in the oncoming pickup truck made sure I had even less. She crossed the white line and blocked the shoulder with her truck as she bore down on me. At first, I thought she did it by mistake. But, when our eyes met and she scowled, I knew she had ill intent. I jumped out of the way and watched in disbelief as she sped by in a rage. Apparently, this woman was having herself a *real bad* day and looking to take it out on someone.

Despite the distance I was running (and the latest attempt on my life), I seemed to get stronger as the day wore on. I guess there's something to be said for working under pressure and challenging yourself … and running for your life.

I ended up reaching the gas station and my car about 15 minutes before sunset. Although I did have a little quad discomfort during the day, all in all, my legs felt pretty darn good. The previous few days I struggled with nagging injuries and my mileage was down. But today, I put in 27.1 miles (the most I've ever run) and felt better than I had in a long time.

Day 67 (11/13/14): Harleyville, SC to Walterboro, SC [24.8 miles]

After checking out of the motel this morning, I drove to the gas station in Harleyville where I left off. The plan for the day was to leave my car there and run about 25 miles to Walterboro, where I'd meet my friend Megan Haskins who recently relocated to South Carolina. Megan would then drive me back to my car, and I'd follow her an hour and half south to her house in Bluffton where I'm staying the next several days. It was a lot of driving, but well worth it. By staying with Megan, I'd have a home base while I'm in the area and rides each day. Plus, I'd have some much-needed social interaction.

As soon as I began running, I could tell I didn't have much energy. No surprise really, I had run over 27 miles in the past 24 hours. I figured I'd have to consume extra energy bars and Gu Energy Gels to get through the day. But it was alright; I had gotten a decent start time-wise, so I wasn't under any pressure today. That's the beauty of an untimed event. I just need to get my miles in. It doesn't matter how long it takes.

During the early part of the day, Route 15 was like it was at the end of yesterday's run, a narrow tree-lined road with a minute shoulder. Not the best running course or the most inspiring scenery. The good thing was, I didn't come across any evil old women in pickup trucks. At least I had that going for me.

Not far along, I got a call from my good friend Matt Platania. Matt was excited to hear how things have been going and listened with great interest as I brought him up to speed on everything. He was enthusiastic and encouraging, even when I whined about my nagging injuries (which, as you know, I tend to do). By the time our conversation ended, I was ready to conquer the day, though I might have worn him out.

I then ran past a home with Old West lawn ornaments galore. In truth, describing them simply as lawn ornaments doesn't do them justice. There were life-size cut-out silhouettes of a stagecoach being pulled by horses and cowboys on horseback roping a stallion. On the front gate of the property were mounted steer skulls, wagon wheels, and horseshoes. Yet, most impressive (and entertaining) was the horse mailbox. The actual box was made to look like a cartoon horse with painted eyes, a grinning mouth, and ears attached. Its body was made out of an old-fashioned metal milk jug and even had a saddle sitting atop. Only in America!

Around 1pm, Route 15 took me over a small swamp with cypress trees and cypress knees protruding from the water. The sight stopped me in my tracks. It wasn't as though I'd never seen a swamp before, but this one was covered in what appeared to be duckweed, giving the water an opaque olive green surface. It looked as though you could walk across it. Of course, I knew

Running The Coast For A Cure

better. One step in and I'd be soaked, and likely short a few toes courtesy of the reptiles lurking within those strange, murky waters.

Minutes later, I ran past a picturesque (and seemingly safer) waterscape with an assortment of trees around a small pond. The leaves of the trees displayed dynamic fall colors not unlike what I'd seen in New England. However, this scene had a distinct southern flair with Spanish moss hanging from the branches and vibrant greens in the vegetation below.

Later in the day, a seemingly harmless little pooch went bonkers when I ran past the house he was guarding. As he charged toward me with wild eyes, I realized something about him wasn't right. He didn't just look angry, he looked *insane*. I knew there was no reasoning with this one. I went right to the mace and sprayed it in the air. He gave it a whiff, snarled, and kept coming (he may have sneered at me as well). I sprayed it again. The deranged doggie responded with more of the same. It was like he was immune to the stuff. Finally, I unleashed everything I had until he backed off ... then I got the heck out of there as fast as I could.

No day is complete without its fair share of aches and pains (and grumbling about it). Today it was pain on the right side of my back, which (sad to say) I was kind of getting used to. Yet, what had me more concerned was the right ankle discomfort I developed late in the day. Keep in mind, it was just minor discomfort, but I had no idea what had caused it. It was something I needed to keep an eye on ... like everything else.

Around 3:30pm, Megan spotted me running down Route 15 and pulled over in front of Pee-Dee's Tires & Wheels (not to be confused with the Great Pee Dee River ... don't laugh, it's a Southern thing). It wasn't the ending location we had planned, but it was within the limits of Walterboro and as good a place to stop as any.

After Meagan and I caught up with each other, she drove me back to my car in Harleyville. I then followed her back to her house in Bluffton. Like I said, it was a lot of driving, but it was a pleasure to be in the company of a friend. It was also reassuring to have someone looking out for me should I need help, especially if I run into – or get run over by – any evil old women ... and no, I don't think I'll be getting over that any time soon.

Day 68 (11/14/14): Walterboro, SC to Yemassee, SC [24.5 miles]

After sleeping in and enjoying a relaxing morning, Megan followed me to the town of Yemassee. I parked my car at a restaurant in town so it would be there when I finished my run. I then hopped in Megan's car, and she drove me back to Pee-Dee's in Walterboro.

When I began my run, it was close to 11am. Even though it was chilly when I left Megan's house, I assumed that the temperature would be warm by the time I got going. Unfortunately for me, it wasn't. It was in the low 50s, which, after the warm temps of the past few days, came as a bit of a shock. I guess it wouldn't have been that big of a deal had the sun been out, but it was nowhere to be seen.

Even so, I did have a new pair of Brooks Glycerin running shoes on my feet. Thanks again to Charm City Run in Annapolis for providing yet another pair, and to my mom for shipping them and the homemade cookies to Megan's house. I know I've said it before, but new running shoes make a world of difference (as do homemade cookies).

Not long after getting started, I reached Walterboro proper and took to the sidewalk that ran through the city past stores, restaurants, and other businesses.

Al DeCesaris

Obviously, running on a sidewalk is much safer than running on the road with speeding cars and trucks. However, a typical concrete sidewalk is a much harder surface than asphalt. Maybe I couldn't tell as much a thousand miles ago, but I sure can these days.

On the far side of Walterboro, I veered onto Route 17 and soon found myself back in rural land. This stretch of 17 was another narrow country road with one lane going in each direction and no shoulder. I'd complain, but after all the country roads I'd run the past couple of months (and all the complaining I've already done) I've pretty much grown accustomed to them.

I then came to an area with a packed gravel path alongside the roadway. It was a safe and soft surface to run on, superior to both the road and the sidewalk of earlier. Although it didn't last long, it was a welcome respite from the speeding vehicles and the hard concrete.

In the early afternoon, I got a call from Shawn Vernon, an old family friend. Shawn is from Maryland, but now lives in South Florida, along my route. He let me know that he could host me and help with rides when I come through his area. It was a generous offer, one that I planned to take him up on. Although it did seem premature to make arrangements in South Florida. I still had a long way to go. However, based on the number of miles I've covered lately, in three weeks or so I'd be in South Florida. I guess it wasn't too soon after all.

Around 2:30pm, I came to a stretch of road that was flat and straight and had Cypress trees extending over

Running The Coast For A Cure

the roadway, obscuring the daylight. With a small, yet hopeful point of light in the distance, it was a scene of serene beauty and inspiration. Just add an uplifting quote and, voila, you'd have a motivational poster.

A couple of hours later, I reached Yemassee. It's a small town with a population of about 1,000 people located in the heart of the Lowcountry, the low-lying region along South Carolina's coast. I wasn't sure if it was the new shoes or what, but when I reached my car, I felt like I could keep running. Not bad considering I had just completed a 24.5-mile day.

That evening, I went to a spa Megan recommended for a massage. It had been two months and about 1,200 miles since my last one, so it was long overdue. However, what should have been a relaxing and rejuvenating experience ended up being a disaster. For some strange reason, halfway through the massage the masseuse put her elbow or knee (or perhaps a pitchfork) into the back of my left knee and thrust forward with vicious force. It caused excruciating pain and left me whimpering. I ended up leaving that place in a whole lot worse shape than when I got there.

I finally made it through a day without any injuries, and I end up getting hurt at the spa. What are the odds?

Day 69 (11/15/14): Yemassee, SC to Hardeeville, SC [25.3 miles]

It was another late start. And not just because I'm not a morning person, though that did play a part in it. What really ate into my time was trying to find a place to leave my car. The best my family had come up with was a location in Hardeeville 29 miles from my starting point.

After that awful experience last night with the masseuse, an effort that ambitious wasn't happening. So, Megan and I drove up and down Route 17 (the desolate tree-lined road Google Maps recommended I take) looking for a place to park my car. After careful searching, we spotted a clearing on the side of the road by train tracks and a swamp (Bagshaw Swamp). I figured it was the best place we'd find so I left my car there with a note on the windshield that read, "I'm doing a charity run. Be back shortly. Please don't tow." I was somewhat optimistic that the note would save my car from the impoundment lot, though not convinced.

It was another chilly day with temperatures in the low 50s. It was also windy. Not my favorite combo, but the sun was out, making the weather (and my ill-advised parking decision) seem a whole lot better.

Also helping matters was wearing another new pair of Brooks Glycerin running shoes. And I had a third new

Al DeCesaris

pair, Saucony Triumph ISO, for tomorrow. Obviously, when Charm City Run said they were going to support the cause, they meant it.

Now with all the new shoes (and both pairs of Brooks Glycerins being the same color), I'll need to remember to keep track of which pair I wear on which day and how many miles I'm putting on them. As I've mentioned before, it's important to keep track of the shoes' mileage so I don't run them (or myself) into the ground. Although some may disagree, after running roughly two-thirds of the way down the East Coast, I'm convinced that rotating my shoes and retiring them when they reach a certain mileage mark has helped keep my injuries to a minimum. And if I'm right, can you imagine what kind of condition I'd be in if I didn't rotate them?

At the start of the day's run, I passed the Yemassee train depot and got onto State Road S-7-3. It's an absurdly narrow road winding through dense woodland that had me wondering if two cars could fit on it at the same time. Lucky for me, not many cars came by while I was on it, so my question was never put to the test. It wasn't until I reached the spot where routes 17 and 21 meet that things opened up ... and got interesting.

Although I could smell it long before I got to it, when I caught sight of the burnt-out police cruiser being hauled away, I couldn't believe my eyes. Megan and I had seen police vehicles racing around with their lights flashing as we made our way to Yemassee, though we had no idea what was going on. Well, whatever had gone down, it must have been one heck of a crazy situation.

Running The Coast For A Cure

As I ran southwest on Route 17, I kept looking for some indication of what happened, but saw nothing. It was killing me that I didn't know, though perhaps it was better I didn't. The last couple of times my curiosity was piqued, I found out there was a ghost haunting the bed and breakfast I was staying at, and that two people died (the previous night!) in the motel room next to me. So yeah, I think it's best I leave this one alone.

About two miles farther, Route 17 merged with Interstate 95. At that point, I got onto a parallel road that ran along I-95. I followed it through Coosawhatchie and into Ridgeland. I then returned to Route 17 and followed it south toward Hardeeville. Because Megan and I had driven that stretch of 17 earlier, I knew the rest of the way was desolate, undeveloped woodland devoid of lights. This presented a problem because the late start had left me short on time. If I didn't pick up the pace, I wouldn't get back to my car before the sun went down. I cranked up the music and started running with urgency.

Over the next hour, I made great time and covered a lot of ground. However, as I ran, I tweaked both my right ankle and left hamstring behind the knee. Neither problem seemed serious, though they did force me to slow my pace.

Around 4:30pm, I ran through another area where the branches of the trees closed in over the roadway, creating a tunnel-like effect. It looked similar to what I'd seen yesterday, though these trees were live oaks, and their tentacle-like branches were dripping with Spanish moss and backlit by the late afternoon sun. Although I knew I couldn't linger, I paused for a moment and marveled at the natural beauty of it. My route today hadn't offered much, but *this* was a sight to see.

Despite my ailing ankle and hamstring, I managed to cover my miles and make it to Bagshaw Swamp just as the sun set. Even more impressive, my car was still there. I actually had the odds on it getting towed at 75%. Sometimes, it's good to be wrong.

That evening I enjoyed a nice home-cooked meal, compliments of Megan. I also enjoyed some *peaceful* rest and relaxation (i.e. no torturous injury-producing massages). And when the day was done, I went to bed happy knowing that tomorrow I'd put this dull and desolate (and, at times, dangerous) state behind me.

Day 70 (11/16/14): Hardeeville, SC to Savannah, GA [24 miles]

After another not so early morning, Megan followed me to the day's ending point, a motel near Savannah Hilton Head International Airport on the outskirts of Savannah, Georgia. I parked my car there, and Megan drove me back to Bagshaw Swamp.

Although the swamp was "technically" in Hardeeville, it wasn't close to the city. As we drove north along Route 17, I realized I had a long way to go before I got to Hardeeville proper. Not that reaching the city was any significant achievement, my goal for the day was crossing into Georgia (and making it back to my car). Still, it'd be nice to get off of this desolate stretch of road and see some life.

When I got started, the temperature was much warmer than it had been the past couple of days, which was great. Warm weather aside, I did have my right ankle and left hamstring to consider. Last night I spoke to Bryan Springer about both issues (it was his turn to get pestered by yours truly). He recommended (aside from the standard self-administered treatments) that I make sure to really loosen up before starting out today … and that I never go back to that spa again. So being

Al DeCesaris

the good patient that I am, I did some extra stretching and walked for the first several miles.

Another thing I hoped would help my ankle and hamstring (or at least not make them worse), was wearing a different style of shoes. Today, it was the new Saucony Triumph ISOs. I'd never worn Triumphs before and was looking forward to trying them out. Fingers crossed, they'd make for a comfy and painless run.

I ended up covering about six miles before I reached anything resembling a city. In fact, nothing about Hardeeville felt "city" to me. Not that I wasn't happy to be there. Compared to the uninhabited tree-lined stretch of road I'd spent the last couple of hours on (and several hours yesterday), a gas station would have been a welcome sight. Joking aside, Hardeeville was a nice community with wide roads bordered by sidewalks, palm trees, and lamp posts with welcome flags on them. It also had lots of restaurants, shops, and hotels.

Not far into it, Route 17 turned to the left, crossed over I-95 and had me heading away from the "city." It then opened up and became a busy road with two lanes going in each direction and a large grassy median, though no shoulder. Under normal circumstances this would have made things stressful. However, there were a bunch of police cruisers out today, which was great because it kept *most* of the drivers on their best behavior … and me thoroughly entertained as I watched car after car get pulled over for speeding.

After about six or seven miles (and twice as many speeding tickets), I exited onto 170 and found myself in

Running The Coast For A Cure

the Savannah National Wildlife Refuge on a narrow stretch of road called "Alligator Alley." At first the road went through wooded land; but, before I knew it, swampland encroached on each side of me, mere feet away. I was just waiting for an alligator to spring out of the water, clamp its teeth down on me, and pull me into a "death roll." And if you don't know what that means, it's when the alligator would be rolling, and I'd be dying. Lucky for me, I made it to a point where the roadway raised up over the swampland before any hungry 'gators reared their ugly heads.

Farther down the road, I came to the Little Black River. With calm blue waters bordered by fields of honey-gold marsh grass and a few lonely trees, it was a captivating sight. Yet even more impressive was the "Welcome We're glad Georgia's on your mind" sign on the far side of the river.

Georgia was one of the 13 original Colonies, one of the 13 original States, and just so happens to be the 13th state of my run. Random facts and coincidences aside, reaching "The Peach State" meant I only needed to survive the rural back-roads another four or five days before I'd be running along the ocean under the Florida sun and in the home stretch. Granted it was a 437-mile home stretch, but who's counting miles?

Not far past the welcome sign, I came to the Savannah River, and soon after entered the sublime and sultry city of Savannah. I had visited the city years ago and loved it. Trouble was, my route didn't take me through the historic district like I'd hoped. Not getting to

Al DeCesaris

see the cobblestone streets, antebellum architecture, and the famous squares with their monuments, fountains, and Spanish moss-covered live oaks was a real disappointment. Though, as I finished out the day, I reminded myself of the reason I'm here. I'm on a mission, not a tour.

Day 71 (11/17/14): Savannah, GA to Richmond Hill, GA [20.4 miles]

It was an early morning, super early for me. The forecast for the day called for heavy rain starting in the afternoon. I decided to get as many miles in as I could before it started. When I got going the wind was gusting. The temperature though was in the high 60s; so as long as the rain held off, I figured I'd be good.

Yesterday when I finished my run, the road (Route 307) was calm and quiet. This morning, however, 307 had heavy traffic with many wide-load trucks. It also had a much smaller shoulder than I remembered. I thought the stress and frustration of rush hour traffic was exclusive to morning commuters, apparently not.

After an hour of me braving (and, on occasion, dodging) speeding vehicles, the traffic died down and the road opened up. At that point, I was able to take in my surroundings. As I mentioned before, this is Savannah, though not the Savannah I know. Still, there were scenic canals and creeks lined with marsh grass and trees of assorted varieties.

The road then turned left and soon ran into Route 17. This stretch of 17 had two lanes going in each direction and shoulders about two-feet wide. That doesn't sound

Al DeCesaris

like much space, but compared to what I started the day on, it was like having my own private lane.

As the morning wore on, my left hamstring started to bother me. I figured it might be because I didn't stretch out enough before I started. Or I could lay blame where I should, at the hands of that maniacal masseuse. Megan might share a little responsibility as well. She was the one who recommended that spa.

Just before 10am, I passed the Little Ogeechee River and was treated to a fascinating view of the river as it passed under the roadway, then wound back toward it only to swing around and zigzag through a field of marsh grass before disappearing from sight. Not more than an hour later, I ran past the Ogeechee River (this must be the "big" one), though I don't remember being nearly as impressed. In fact, I don't remember much about it at all. I was too preoccupied with the growing discomfort in my hamstring and gathering rain clouds.

Later in the day, I reached Richmond Hill and considered calling it a day. It would have been the safe play considering the way my hamstring felt and the sky looked. Plus, there were several places where I could have held up until Megan arrived to get me, namely Waffle House. I do love my breakfast food. Still, at that point, I was only 17 miles in and hoped to get in a few more. I'm no meteorologist, but from the look of things I figured I had another hour before the storm rolled in, so I forewent the waffles and pressed on.

My atmospheric assessment couldn't have been more wrong. About 20 minutes in, it started to drizzle.

Running The Coast For A Cure

Soon after, the sky opened up on me. Of course, I was a couple of miles past the restaurants and couldn't find cover. I texted Megan asking her to come get me, put on my cheapo red poncho, and started running down the road. The first half mile was kind of fun, but as the rain intensified and the thunder rumbled (and the anxious messages from Megan started to come in), I grew concerned. Without an address and with neither of us knowing the area, we were at a loss as to where I was and how she'd find me. After a lengthy back and forth, I told her to just drive down Route 17 and keep an eye out for me ... I'd be the water-logged fool in the hobo poncho sloshing down the road.

Another problem I faced (as though I needed any more), it was raining so hard the drive there might take Megan the better part of an hour. Not to mention, I was on the other side of 17 and visibility was limited. *Would she even see me when she drove by?* I had to find a place to hold up. It ended up taking a while, but I spotted a gas station/convenience store down the road. I put my head down and raced toward it.

After calling Megan to let her know where I was, I ditched the poncho and went inside for a cold drink and a bite to eat. By the time she arrived, I was sitting under an awning out front of the store sucking down a Gatorade, chomping on a PowerBar, and chilling out like I was having a picnic ... which, in my whacky world out on the road, that's exactly what I was doing, albeit a ridiculously wet one.

Day 72 (11/18/14): Richmond Hill, GA to Townsend, GA [28.7 miles]

Perhaps I bit off more than I could chew, but this morning I set out to cover 28.7 miles, the most thus far. The reason for the big number was that I didn't get in as many miles as I needed to yesterday. Yet, what convinced me to give it a go was knowing that Megan would pick me up wherever I decided to stop.

After getting the thumbs-up to leave my car in the gas station/convenience store parking lot where I left off, I headed out for what I knew would be a very challenging day. Not making things any easier was the temperature. It was in the high 40s (not exactly shorts weather).

A couple of miles in, Route 17, which in this area goes by the name Coastal Highway, went from four lanes down to two and turned into just another narrow country road. I'd been forewarned that most of my miles in Georgia would be through desolate rural nothingness. But calling it "Coastal" Highway … did they have to be so cruel?

Not much farther along, a flatbed truck with a piece of lumber hanging out of the bed came barreling by and almost took my head off. It happened so fast and was so shocking that I wasn't sure what exactly had transpired. Yet, I do know this – had the driver been a couple feet closer to me or had I not gotten off the shoulder at the last second, this all would have ended tragically.

The dangers of my run are something I think about often. Injuries are bad enough, but getting struck by a vehicle (or, in this case, decapitated by a piece of lumber) would be horrific, and not just for me. I'm doing this run for my niece and the entire Sturge-Weber community. The last thing I want to do is bring stress and anxiety into anyone's life. Even though this particular situation was hard to foresee, moving forward, I need to be much more diligent.

About five miles later, I came to a quaint little city called Midway. Midway Congregational Church (AKA Midway Meeting House) and its cemetery immediately caught my eye. The church is a white colonial structure with a central steeple built in the 1790s. The cemetery has, amid its headstones and Spanish moss-covered trees, a monument dedicated to American generals, Daniel Stewart and James Screven, who served during the Revolutionary War.

After leaving Midway, I ran past Blackbeard Creek. It was a scenic waterway, but also a curious one. A stone's throw from the bridge I crossed, stood two rows of old wooden pilings protruding out of the water. *The remnants of a bridge? Maybe an old dam?* One question peaked my curiosity even more – did the name of the creek have any connection to Blackbeard the pirate?

An hour or so later, I reached Riceboro and was able to run on a sidewalk safe from speeding vehicles (and renegade lumber). As I've said before, sidewalk running

Running The Coast For A Cure

can be tough on your body, but after my near-death experience I was all about safety. Plus, with the exception of minor discomfort in my left hamstring and right ankle, I felt pretty good. I figured a few miles on a sidewalk shouldn't be a problem.

Later in the day, I ran past another scenic waterway much like the one I saw earlier. I suppose that stands to reason because it's actually part of Blackbeard Creek. It seems this creek, like me, runs all over the place.

Toward the end of my run, I ran past Blackbeard Creek, again. At that point, I *had* to know why every waterway I came upon had that name and if it had any connection to the notorious English pirate. After studying Google Maps, I realized that each waterway was interconnected and therefore all part of Blackbeard Creek. I later learned that the creek is named after Edward Teach, the ship captain of the "Queen Anne's Revenge." And, yes ... he was Blackbeard.

Not long after, I reached the Eulonia Motel, the day's ending point. Megan then picked me up and drove me back to my car. It was time for me to move on down the road, so Megan and I said our goodbyes. Although she wasn't born and raised in the south, I'd put her southern hospitality up against anyone's.

As I drove to my hotel, I thought about what I had just accomplished. For me, running 28.7 miles was an unbelievable achievement, especially considering that a couple of months ago I struggled with 18 – 20 mile runs. Yet, I always believed I could do this. I guess I just needed some time for my legs to catch up to my brain.

Day 73 (11/19/14): Townsend, GA to Brunswick, GA [29 miles]

After a hearty breakfast, I drove to the day's ending point, Family Life Church in Brunswick. There, I met Clint Crews from Walgreens. At this point it probably goes without saying, but when I mention Walgreens it means two things – one: I couldn't find a ride, and two: Anna O'Herren came through for us yet again.

Like all the Walgreens employees who have helped, Clint couldn't have been more supportive. He drove me to the Eulonia Motel where I left off and wished me well. I then started what was to be a 26-mile run.

The plan was to spend the majority of those miles on Route 17. Other than a few turns toward the end of the run, I was pretty much on auto-pilot for the day. Not to say 26 miles is a walk in the park, but after yesterday's super-long run, the number was much more palatable.

It was another cold day with temps in the low 50s, but the sun helped take the edge off. Like yesterday, Route 17 took me through quiet woodland. Usually I would complain about this, especially because the shoulder was extremely narrow. But I could run on a flat grassy area to the side of the shoulder if I needed to get off the road. Plus, I had Frank Herbert's epic science fiction novel (audio edition, of course), *Dune*, to preoccupy me.

About 10 miles in, I reached Darien. The city is situated on the water with shops, restaurants, and lots of live oaks and palm trees. Whether it was the change of scenery or the fact that I felt good physically, I made it through Darien in no time. I must confess, it was *only* about a mile long so that might explain it. As I crossed the bridge over the Darien River and left the city, I had a great view of Darien's little waterfront with its boardwalk, covered seating area, and docks with shrimp boats.

About three quarters of a mile farther, I crossed the Butler River. The next mile or so took me past marshland before coming to the Altamaha River. A half mile beyond that, I reached the Altamaha River, again. It's confusing I know, but it could have been worse. They all could have been part of Blackbeard Creek.

When I got past all the rivers and bridges, 17 took me through a lonely, yet striking stretch of road with fields of chartreuse and honey-gold sawgrass surrounding a group of trees. It seemed the Spanish moss hanging from their limbs was consuming them. Still, the proud trees remained steadfast.

A little later, the navigation lady interrupted the feature presentation (which is riveting by the way) to tell me, in that cunning voice of hers, to turn off of 17 and onto an adjacent back road. I wasn't sure what her reasoning was, but a quick look at Google Maps confirmed a shorter route to the day's ending point. So, I

Day 74 (11/20/14): Brunswick, GA to Woodbine, GA [25 miles]

The last couple of nights I had the good fortune of staying in a nice hotel compliments of Will Futch. If we had awards for those who have helped this charity event, Will would undoubtedly get one of the top honors, as would Anna O'Herren. As though she needed to do anything more to validate that distinction, today she came through yet again by finding me a ride.

After checking out of the hotel, I drove to the day's ending point, Captain Stan's Smokehouse in Woodbine, where I met Jimmy from Walgreens. I know I've said it before, but every Walgreens employee who has helped has been incredibly kind and supportive.

Before heading out, I went inside Captain Stan's to make sure it was okay for me to leave my car in their parking lot. I ended up talking to a young woman named Ashley who told me it would be fine and pointed out where in the lot I should park my car. She then flashed a warm smile and wished me well.

Jimmy drove me back to the church in Brunswick where I left off. As soon as I started out, I knew something wasn't right. Toward the end of yesterday's run, as I raced headlong against the setting sun, I felt a twinge in my right forefoot. I figured it was just a bad step and convinced myself it was nothing to worry about. However, the way it felt today had me thinking I might have done damage to it … and that had me very concerned.

On the bright side, it was warm today and the sun was shining. About a mile down the road, I came to a bridge that took me over Fancy Bluff Creek onto Blythe Island. It was a small island with marshland close to the water's edge and woodland in the interior. After I crossed the island, I took another bridge over the creek and soon merged back onto Route 17.

At that point, my right foot was in terrible pain and I decided to walk. Usually when things get bad, I walk for a while and the pain subsides. Today, however, that didn't work. Not only did the pain not subside, it was intense even while walking. Was it the increased mileage the past two days? Was it the frantic pace I kept at the end of yesterday's run? Or was it an overuse injury that I would have developed regardless? Whatever the cause, I feared I might have severely injured it. I stopped, took off my shoe to massage my foot, and considered calling for help.

A couple of days back, I might have called Megan to pick me up. But I was well south of her now. I could have called the local police department and asked for a ride. But I really didn't want to do that. During the entire run, I had never done anything like that, not even when my shin splints were at their worst. I needed to work through this myself … and I needed to get my miles in. So, I laced up my shoe and got back out there.

Running The Coast For A Cure

There wasn't much to see on that stretch of 17, not much at all. It was a straight, flat, tree-lined road with a few houses here and there. As I shuffled along, the pain (now extending into the arch of my foot) and the monotony of the road wore me down. Eventually, the pain got so unbearable, I decided to start running again. I figured it couldn't get much worse. I'm not sure about the logic of that, but I might have been onto something because I didn't notice much of a difference.

When I reached the community of Waverly, the navigation lady tried to get me to take the rail trail that ran parallel to 17. Based on the fact that vehicles were prohibited on it, the trail probably would have been safer for me. But no way was I getting off 17 and onto a trail that might dead-end like those roads did yesterday. No, that *definitely* wasn't happening.

The long stretches of walking I did earlier cost me all kinds of time. I soon realized that in order to reach Woodbine before nightfall I would have to pick up the pace considerably. So, I dug down deep and began an unsteady dash. It was sloppy and painful, but it did the job. A bit before sundown, I crossed the Satilla River and reached the street lights and sidewalks of Woodbine.

When I got back to Captain Stan's and my car, I found a note on the windshield from Ashley that read, "enjoy your journey." Even though it had been a long, difficult, and painful day (and pretty much has been that way from the very beginning), I *am* enjoying my journey and am honored and proud to be doing it.

281

Day 75 (11/21/14): Woodbine, GA to Yulee, FL [25.3 miles]

After two and a half months of overcoming obstacles and injuries, today I would *finally* reach Florida, and top the 1,500-mile mark. I must admit, there were times I wondered if I'd make it. But there I was, closing in on "The Sunshine State" and about to kick-off the final chapter – the final state – of this epic journey.

In the late morning, I met Ryan from Walgreens at the day's ending point, Dollar General in Yulee. That's ride number 15 Anna has arranged; which begs the question, how on earth am I ever going to repay her for all of her help?

Ryan got me back to Captain Stan's in Woodbine, just before 11am. It was a bit of a late start. But, after yesterday's struggles, I needed some extra rest which seemed to help. I felt much better today, even if I wasn't 100% … though, with the exception of the first day of the run, when have I ever been 100%?

A few minutes after I got going, I found myself in humdrum rural land. Route 17 had given me more than my fair share of this as of late. I was hoping today the scenery would be different, but to my disappointment, it was more of the same. One good thing though, the weather was nice with temps in the low 60s and the sun was shining.

About an hour into my run, I developed pain in the arch of my right foot similar to what I experienced yesterday. It felt like the muscles spasmed, not unlike a dehydration cramp. Now, I don't know if that's what it was, but I sure hoped it was nothing more than that.

Oddly enough, the forefoot pain I experienced yesterday wasn't as noticeable. Not that it wasn't bothering me, it just wasn't *as bad* today. I assumed that the forefoot and the arch issues were related, but now wondered if they were two separate problems. If so, maybe the arch pain *was* the result of dehydration and the forefoot pain was just a bruise or something minor. This was my cup-is-half-full mindset, which I'm sure was just getting carried away with itself. Still, I liked the positive thoughts and decided to run with them (literally and figuratively). Even when a rock shot out from under the tire of a truck and nailed me in the groin, I stayed upbeat … although I did keel over and almost threw up.

About 10 miles in, I reached a small city called Kingsland. While passing through, I stopped at a convenience store for a Gatorade. If dehydration was causing my foot problems, I figured I'd better get some fluids and minerals into my system. And if it wasn't … well then, I had a real problem, and I might as well enjoy a cold drink and a break.

About four miles past Kingsland, I came to St. Marys River. According to Google Maps, the river was the dividing line between Georgia and Florida. Now, you'd think I would have raced over the bridge as fast as I could out of sheer excitement. Well, I did race over it, but more out of fear than anything else. Although the bridge wasn't long, it was extremely narrow with no shoulder whatsoever, and barely wide enough for two cars to pass each other. Nothing like adding the element of danger right before the prize.

Lucky for me, I made it across the bridge and into "The Sunshine State" before any vehicles came by. Just beyond the bridge was the sight of all sights, the "Welcome to Florida" sign. When I saw it, a wave of emotions overcame me, and I got teary-eyed. Having run all those miles through 13 states and now to be in the final state of this improbable journey was hard to comprehend ... but it was truly awesome.

Al DeCesaris at the Florida state line.

Al DeCesaris

The next 30 minutes were filled with a few dozen state-sign-selfies (I had to get the picture *just* right) and text messages and calls to family and friends. I wanted everyone to know *I had made it!*

After that, it was a couple more hours of boring nothing-to-see Route 17. But I didn't care. I was on cloud nine and reveling in the excitement of it all.

As I made my way to Yulee and my car, I reflected on what I had just accomplished. The more I thought about it, the more amazed I became. Although I still have a long way to go, no matter what happens moving forward … I ran from Maine to Florida! … from the East Coast's northernmost state to its southernmost state. That is an unbelievable achievement, one that no one can ever take away from me, and one that would not have been possible if not for my little inspiration Jenna giving me purpose to fight on her behalf.

Day 76 (11/22/14): Yulee, FL to Jacksonville, FL [23.6 miles]

This morning I met Simon at the day's ending point, the Scottish Inn in Jacksonville. Simon was my driver for the day (and, yes, he's another Walgreens employee). Every time someone from Walgreens comes to my aid, I'm amazed. Keep in mind, just because Anna puts out the request doesn't mean this is something the employees are obligated to do. These individuals freely volunteer their time to help the cause. It's remarkable and I couldn't be more appreciative.

Simon dropped me off at the Dollar General in Yulee where I left off. The temperature was in the mid 60s and the sky had the look of rain. It had me thinking the forecast, which called for *late* afternoon showers, might not be so accurate and the rain might come much earlier. I knew I needed to keep a brisk pace to get my miles in before it started. I also knew it would be a real challenge with the foot issues I'd been battling.

I followed Route 17 out of Yulee and into the countryside. To my disappointment, the Florida landscape wasn't teeming with orange orchards and palm trees as I'd hoped. The scenery looked a lot like it did every other day as of late – undeveloped, uninhabited, tree-lined monotony.

Al DeCesaris

About three and a half miles in, I crossed the Nassau River and reached the city of Jacksonville. The funny thing was, there were no signs whatsoever that I was in the city, or any city for that matter, other than the actual sign on the side of the road that said so. Jacksonville's city limits must have an extensive reach because from what I could see, it was rural land for miles.

Despite the mundane surroundings, I made good time the early part of the run. It all went south, however, when the arch of my right foot started acting up. Again, it was the "dehydration cramp" type of pain. After dealing with this issue the past several days, I was starting to doubt that dehydration had anything to do with it. Still, whenever the pain flared up, I stopped running and drank water from my hydration pack. I don't know how much to credit the water (I imagine the breaks were what really helped), but the pain did tend to subside, albeit temporarily.

As I moved south along 17, it got more developed and populated. It wasn't a metropolis, mind you, but I could see how they justified calling this area part of the city. After spending so many long days in rural lands, I looked forward to seeing the organized chaos of a city.

As my excitement grew, so did the pain in my foot. At that point, I had to stop kidding myself and face reality. The pain was not the result of dehydration. I had an injury, most likely affecting the tissue that connects the heel to the toes and supports the arch. I later learned that an injury of this sort is known as plantar fasciitis, and can be caused by running on surfaces that are too

Running The Coast For A Cure

hard or uneven, or by running for extended periods of time; check, check, and check.

Just before 1pm, I crossed the Trout River. Soon after, it started to rain, and I took cover under the roof of a defunct business. Under normal circumstances, I would have been frustrated by this, but my foot was in such bad shape I welcomed the break. I pulled off my shoe and massaged my foot, hoping to alleviate the pain. The trouble was, neither my foot nor the weather cooperated – the pain persisted, and the rain stopped. I grudgingly put on my shoe and continued on, though I decided it was best to walk the rest of the way.

Around 2pm, I reached downtown Jacksonville with its high-rise buildings, hotels, restaurants, theaters, and the anticipated chaos of the city. However, there were few people around and little action. It was a disappointment. But I guess, I'll cut Jacksonville a break; it was a gloomy, rainy November day. Even at my lethargic pace, I was through the downtown area before I knew it and crossing the St. Johns River, which bisects the city. A mile or so beyond the river, I reached the Scottish Inn, closing out a painful and uneventful day.

I then drove to Ponte Vedra Beach to the home of Susie Duvall, who is hosting me for a few days. Susie is the sister of my cousin's wife, which makes her ... the sister of my cousin's wife. I had seen her at family functions a bunch of times over the years, but we didn't know each other well. Well, after a warm greeting and a fantastic home-cooked meal (and a few episodes of Seinfeld and Friends), we were as thick as thieves.

Day 78 (11/24/14): Jacksonville, FL to St. Augustine, FL [26.2 miles]

When you're doing something as physically and mentally demanding as running down the entire East Coast, on occasion you find yourself looking for a reason to take a day off. Well, yesterday prayers were answered, and I got to enjoy a relaxing and rejuvenating rain day. I must confess, it only rained a little while, and had I run I might have gotten in most of my miles. But when I heard they were calling for rain, I didn't focus on the details. I just saw the forecast as an opportunity to get in some long overdue and much needed recovery time.

However, my "rain day" wasn't just about recovering. I caught up on my zzz's as well (you know how much I love my sleep). Later in the day, I got a haircut, and had the good fortune of meeting Renee. She not only gave me a superb cut (and had me looking dapper, if I do say so myself), but she gave me loads of encouragement and impressed upon me the importance of what I'm doing. I can't stress enough what it means to receive that kind of support. It motivates me and validates what I'm striving to achieve.

Renee and I discovered we both had been inspired by the documentary film *Running the Sahara*, which

Al DeCesaris

chronicles Ray Zahab, Charlie Engle, and Kevin Lin's 4,300-mile expedition across the Sahara Desert. For Renee, their extraordinary accomplishment brought her hope during a difficult time. For me, it planted the seed of this journey, and coupled with the advice and encouragement I later received from Ray Zahab, helped me believe I could accomplish it.

I then went to a local running store and bought a pair of Hoka One One Conquests. I know I wasn't due for a new pair of shoes, but I *was* due for a new pair of Hokas. I'd been Hoka-less for over a month now. With the development of plantar fasciitis in my right foot, I wanted to do everything I could to ease the stress on it.

That evening, Susie, her sister Chris, and Chris' husband Jim took me to dinner. Although I would have been just as happy with another of Susie's home-cooked meals (did I mention she's a fantastic cook?), it was fun to spend an evening out with such wonderful people.

Today there was no rain in the forecast, not even a drizzle, so I was back at it with my new Hokas on my feet. After a scrumptious breakfast compliments of "semi-cousin" Susie, she drove me to the Scottish Inn in Jacksonville where I last left off. The plan for the day was to run down Route 1 roughly 26 miles to Grace Community Church in St. Augustine.

When I got started, the temperature was in the high 70s, and expected to climb into the 80s, making it one of the warmest days yet. Route 1 through this part of Jacksonville has two lanes going in each direction, a

Running The Coast For A Cure

large grass median, and tons of businesses along both sides of the road. The first few miles I had a sidewalk to run on, but after that the majority of my miles were on the busy roadway just a few feet from a steady flow of traffic. The good news was, my right foot felt okay. In fact, it felt pretty darn good, as did the rest of me. It was the first day in a long time I could say that. Raising the question, "The $64,000 Question," was it the new Hokas or the day of rest?

Although I prefer the heat over the cold any day of the week, today it was warmer and more humid than I was used to. I usually don't go through all my water, so this morning I only filled my hydration pack three quarters of the way. Of course, I ended up regretting that decision. I went through my water quickly and after a while the humidity started to get the better of me. Lucky for me, I came upon a convenience store and was able to refill my hydration pack. Yet, I may not be so fortunate next time. Moving forward, I have to make sure I'm better prepared for the Florida heat and humidity.

I knew I had a lot of miles to cover before I got through Jacksonville, but I didn't realize I'd be spending the majority of my day there. I later learned that it's the largest city by area in the contiguous United States, which stands to reason considering all that rural land I had to suffer through yesterday.

Later in the day, I got past the strip malls and congestion of the "city" only to return to undeveloped land and the monotonous boredom that comes with it. The rural surroundings came as a surprise and a bit of a

293

letdown, especially so because I'd been anticipating (and looking forward to) running along the Atlantic Ocean. I guess I'll have to wait at least another day before actually "running the coast."

Despite the heat and humidity (and the tiresome scenery toward the end of the day), I managed to get all my miles in (26.2 of them, the official marathon distance) without dehydration taking hold and without any pain or discomfort in my foot. Here's to hoping tomorrow will be another pain-free day. And if it's not too much to ask, I'd prefer if it's a lot less humid and a lot more scenic.

Day 79 (11/25/14): St. Augustine, FL to St. Augustine, FL [23.6 miles]

After starting the day with another mouthwatering meal, I loaded up my car (it was time to move on) and followed Susie to the day's ending point, or so we thought. I'm not sure how it happened, but we somehow ended up back at Grace Community Church, yesterday's ending point. For the sake of time, I decided to leave my car there and Susie offered to pick me up at the end of the day and drive me back to it.

The forecast for the day called for heavy rain, though when I got started it was only drizzling. Now, if you're wondering why I was out there when they predicted rain, so am I. Bottom line, the remainder of my schedule has been set and to reach Key Largo by the projected finish date I couldn't afford to take another day off.

Although I didn't need my poncho right then, I decided to put it on so I wouldn't have to fiddle with it when the time came. Even with cooler temps (it was in the high 60s), it was a sweatbox under that thing. I realize I could have taken it off, but I figured the minute I did the sky would open up on me.

The first hour or so I had to suffer through mundane scenery again. But then the landscape changed, becoming more developed and populated. Around eight miles in, I left Route 1 for SR A1A, the state road that

Al DeCesaris

runs down Florida's east coast almost entirely along the ocean and entered St. Augustine proper.

St. Augustine, also known as the "Ancient City," was founded in 1565 and is the oldest continuously inhabited European-established settlement in the continental United States. As I made my way into the historic district, I ran past two statues of conquistadors: one represented the Spanish explorer who led the first European expedition to Florida, Juan Ponce de Leon, and the other the Spanish admiral and explorer who founded the city, Don Pedro Menendez de Aviles. I then passed a couple of the city's kitschy tourist attractions, the Old Jail and the Fountain of Youth, before running past the Colonial Spanish Quarter and Castillo de San Marcos, a Spanish-built fort dating to the late 1600s.

Just past the Castillo, I came to the Bridge of Lions, a bascule bridge with two marble lions standing guard at the foot of it. After snapping pictures of the stalwart sentinels, I took the bridge over the Matanzas River onto Anastasia Island. A1A then turned south, and I began my run down Florida's coast. (FYI, this is the "running the coast" portion of my run I have been waiting for!)

Along the road were restaurants, shops, businesses, and behind them homes. Although I couldn't see the ocean yet, I knew it was there. I could smell it in the air. I followed A1A past St. Augustine's black-and-white striped Lighthouse and the Alligator Farm Zoological Park, then through the neighborhood of St. Augustine Beach. Along this stretch, it was less commercialized. However, there were still no ocean views from the road.

Running The Coast For A Cure

As I continued down A1A through the neighborhood of Butler Beach and into Crescent Beach, I caught a glimpse of the ocean at last. It was more like a glimpse of homes perched atop sand dunes in front of the ocean. Even so, it was all good with me because that heavy rain I'd been concerned about wasn't falling.

I peeled off the poncho with both pleasure and irritation. Like a fool, I'd worn that glorified trash bag all day when I didn't need to. However, I must have jinxed myself by taking it off because right about then it began to rain. It wasn't hard at first and left me believing I could still make it to the day's ending point before it really started coming down. Of course, I did have the security of knowing that if I experienced any problems, I could call Susie and have her pick me up sooner.

Well, my assessment was *way* off. Within 10 minutes, the sky was as dark as night, and the rain was falling … and I was hunkered down under a tree, putting in that call to Susie. Unfortunately, it was going to take her about an hour to reach me, so I figured I might as well keep running until she got to the area. Plus, if I kept a decent pace, with another hour of running I still might reach my ending point.

As I sloshed down the road in my "trusty" poncho, lightning lit up the sky and thunder crashed. Rain I can deal with, but a full-blown thunderstorm with lightning striking all over the place … count me out.

At that point, I was in a residential area and couldn't find cover. Short of knocking on someone's door and begging them to let me in, I was stuck out in the

297

elements. So, I pressed on, running as fast as I could, hoping I'd find cover before a lightning bolt found me.

After some anxiety-filled running, I reached the bridge spanning the Matanzas Inlet. I knew it was a bad idea to be on a bridge during a thunder storm, but just on the other side was the day's ending point, Kangaroo Express gas station/convenience store. Even though I was scared that lightning would strike while I was on the bridge, I didn't like the idea of waiting out in the open on the side of the road either. As I mustered up my courage, I said a quick prayer and a few more while I raced across the steel and concrete structure like my life depended on it (which it very well may have). I don't know if it was my guardian angel protecting me or just blind luck, but I somehow made it over the bridge and into the convenience store without being lit up like a Christmas tree.

Susie arrived soon after and was as excited to see me as I'd been to see the inside of that store. I think she had seriously doubted whether I'd still be breathing when she found me. It stands to reason. This wasn't just a little rain shower. This was a severe thunderstorm. I was very, *very* fortunate to get through it safely.

As Susie drove me back to my car, I made sure to thank her for the hospitality (and all the tasty meals). She then thanked me for not getting struck by lightning. Apparently, having to call my family and share that kind of news wasn't how she wanted to end her watch over her semi-cousin.

Day 80 (11/26/14): St. Augustine, FL to Ormond-by-the-Sea, FL [25.5 miles]

After breakfast, I drove from my motel in Palm Coast (where I stayed last night and am staying tonight) to the day's ending point, Lagerhead's Bar and Grill in Ormond-by-the-Sea. The seaside watering hole is located right across the street from the ocean and has a fantastic view. Although I would have loved to make a day of it there taking in the ocean view and some liquified carbs, I needed to get miles in, all 25.5 of them.

My volunteer driver for the day was Irv from Walgreens. (For those keeping a tally, that's ride number 17 that Anna has arranged, which includes the driving she and her husband did while I stayed with them.) As Irv drove me to yesterday's ending point, I told him about the cause. He was very interested to hear all about it and supportive of my efforts. I then learned that Irv does a lot of charity work himself and could relate to what I'm doing. Before dropping me off, he invited me to join him and his family for Thanksgiving dinner. It was a generous offer, one that I would have taken him up on had I not already made plans.

When I started the day's run, it was gloomy and cold, though compared to yesterday's tempestuous weather it was a lovely day. And it was supposed to get even

Al DeCesaris

better. The forecast for the afternoon was partly sunny with temps in the high 50s.

A quarter of a mile down the road, A1A extended over marshy ground, and the trees to the left side of the road gave way to grass-covered dunes, a sandy beach, and the Atlantic Ocean. In the air a lone seagull flew, and on the shore the occasional wave crashed. Even with a backdrop of gray clouds, it was a beautiful sight.

The road then curved to the right and drew close to Matanzas River, which is part of the Atlantic Intercoastal Waterway, a navigable route that runs along the East Coast from the mouth of the Chesapeake Bay to the Florida Keys. The Intercoastal is impressive in its own right and should provide spectacular scenery as I run down the coast.

The road then drew back to the left and before I knew it, I could see the ocean again. But it was more than just seeing it, the road ran *right along* the Atlantic with nothing between the pavement and the surf other than grassy dunes and the sandy beach. If I had a beach towel and a little free time, who knows ... though that should probably wait for a sunny day, and one when I don't have 25 miles to run.

Next, A1A took me past an area with oceanfront homes and beyond that, condo complexes. The road then veered to the right and led me through Washington Oaks Gardens State Park. Along this stretch, the roadway was lined with live oaks, palm trees, and dense vegetation of saw palmettos.

Running The Coast For A Cure

On the south side of the parkland, I stepped off the roadway and onto a trail that snaked through dense vegetation under a canopy of live oaks covered in Spanish moss. It was like Deep South meets the tropics, though some may just call it North Florida.

As the day wore on, the sun came out and the temperature rose. What had started as a cold, dreary day turned into a beautiful, bright one.

Around 2pm, I reached Flagler Beach, a picturesque seaside community with a fishing pier, shops, and restaurants with ocean views. As I ran past a restaurant with outdoor seating, an attractive young woman sitting at one of the tables said hello to me and smiled. I was so caught off guard, I didn't know what to say. By the time I came up with a decent response, I was a quarter of a mile past the restaurant. Despite my tongue-tied performance, her smile put a spring in my step. Never underestimate the power of a woman's smile.

Later in the day, as I ran past Gamble Rogers Memorial State Recreation Area, I saw out of the corner of my eye a large cat-like creature. I stopped for a better look, then wished I hadn't. It looked feral and stared me down like I was its next meal. I didn't know what to do: hold my ground, run away as fast as I could, or scream for help. In the end, I scampered off like a mouse being chased by a cat. Although in this scenario, the frightened animal had mace in his hand and his finger on the trigger.

A few miles later, I passed a patrolman and told him what I'd seen. He said it was probably a bobcat as they are known to inhabit the area. He then told me I was lucky. Now, I wasn't sure if he meant I was lucky to have seen a bobcat … or lucky the bobcat didn't attack me.

Toward the end of the day, I ran past another restaurant with outdoor seating, and a man asked where I was headed. Without breaking stride, I told him Key Largo and that I'd started in Maine. His eyes widened and his jaw dropped. Another patron shouted, "you go, you!" His cheer had me laughing and brought a big smile to my face. Encouragement, even when it's a bit nonsensical, is pretty cool.

Around 5pm, I reached Lagerhead's, finishing a day that included a bit of everything: an act of kindness from a new friend, an alluring smile from an attractive woman, a panic-stricken bobcat encounter, humorous encouragement from a total stranger, and miles and miles of amazing ocean views.

Day 81 (11/27/14): Ormond-by-the-Sea to New Smyrna Beach, FL [23.5 miles]

Although running 23.5 miles wasn't the way I wanted to spend Thanksgiving Day, I did have plenty to be thankful for. For starters, I was thankful to be in sunny Florida and enjoying the amazing ocean views. I was also thankful to be running without any injuries. And even though I couldn't spend Thanksgiving with my family, I was thankful for their love and support. Most important, I was thankful for my beautiful niece Jenna who inspired me to run on her behalf.

I was also thankful that I'd be spending the next several days with Jeanette and Mitch Ribak. They're the grandparents of an adorable 8-year-old girl named Lola. Like Jenna, Lola suffers with Sturge-Weber syndrome, but isn't letting it keep her down. Neither are Mitch and Jeanette. Since 2007, they've been hosting charity events and have raised significant funds for medical research. Their love for their granddaughter is without measure.

The only negative was I had to wake up at an ungodly hour to get my miles in and still have enough time to drive to Mitch and Jeanette's house and get cleaned up for Thanksgiving dinner. As you know, the early morning hours are no friend of mine, but for turkey, cranberry sauce, and stuffing I could make an exception.

At way-too-early o'clock, Mitch and I met at the day's ending point, Bello Valentino's restaurant in New Smyrna Beach. It was the first time we'd seen each other since meeting last fall at a Kennedy Krieger Institute event. As an aside, during that event Ida was honored for the amazing work she's done raising awareness and funds for Sturge-Weber research (yep, I'm bragging about her; she *is* my one and only sister). As Mitch drove me to my starting point, we caught up with one another and I shared stories of my adventures.

By the time Mitch dropped me off at Lagerhead's, it was around 7:30am. The sun was out, and temps were in the 60s, making for a fantastic day. And, yes, you better believe I was thankful for that as well.

As I ran down A1A through Ormond-by-the-Sea, I watched lazy waves roll onto the shore and morning light dance on calm blue waters. When I got farther south, the buildings alongside the road got bigger and bigger. I wasn't sure where the dividing line was, but somewhere along that stretch, the seaside community of Ormond-by-the-Sea gave way to the city of Ormond Beach. Before long, I found myself surrounded by tall condominium complexes, hotels, restaurants, stores, and other businesses.

A1A then led me into a bigger, busier, and far wilder seaside city, Daytona Beach. Being a top destination for spring-breakers and the home of numerous annual events and festivals, it has the reputation of a party town. Yet, its claim to fame is auto racing. For more than 100 years, due in large part to its hard-packed sand beach that cars can drive on, Daytona Beach has hosted premier auto racing events. Presently, at the Daytona International Speedway, it hosts the "Great American Race," NASCAR's Daytona 500.

Unfortunately (or rather, fortunately), there were no fun events today, and I was able to run without being lured to some wild beach party. After a while, the navigation lady had me heading toward the Intercoastal, which in this area goes by the name Halifax River. I wasn't thrilled to leave A1A, but according to the navigation lady I needed to get over to Route 1. She then directed me onto Broadway Bridge. As I ran the bridge, I was treated to fantastic views of Halifax River and the Daytona skyline. I also enjoyed the intricate mosaics on the bridge, each depicting wildlife native to Florida. I made sure to snap a picture of the one with a bobcat (I'm not sure why; it just called to me).

When I got to the other side, I turned onto Beach Street. Although Beach doesn't run along the beach, it does run along the river and has lots of palm trees as well as shops and cafes. I then passed a marina filled with sail boats and motor boats. Although it was quiet today, I imagine this is a happening area when people aren't home carving turkeys and stuffing their faces.

Soon after, the navigation lady directed me onto Route 1. The next five or six miles took me through commercial areas with nothing of note. It wasn't until the last few miles that the scenery got Thanksgiving-worthy again. Along that stretch, I ran past several bodies of water, or perhaps just one big body of water that was all interconnected (it wouldn't be the first time). Whatever the case, I ran over a series of bridges and enjoyed one spectacular waterscape after another.

Not long after, I arrived at my ending point. I had made decent time, though I still had a bit of a drive before me. Mitch and Jeanette live in Brevard County near Kennedy Space Center, and I reached their house an hour later. When I arrived, Jeanette greeted me warmly. It was great to see her. She's one of those positive, upbeat people that exudes kindness.

After I got cleaned up, we went to the Black Tulip restaurant in Cocoa Village for Thanksgiving dinner. Unfortunately, Lola and her mother Amanda weren't in town, but Jeanette's son Michael and her mother Audrey were with us. Considering a good portion of this run I've been in the middle of nowhere all by myself, I was truly blessed to spend Thanksgiving with Mitch and Jeanette and their wonderful, loving family. It was yet another thing to be thankful for on this day of thanksgiving.

Day 82 (11/28/14): New Smyrna Beach, FL to Mims, FL [30.3 miles]

It was another painfully early morning. Mileage-wise, I had a big day ahead of me. And in the evening Mitch and Jeanette were hosting a fundraising event for the cause at UNO Pizzeria, not far from their house. I *had* to get my miles in by early afternoon to get there in time…. I was the guest of honor, I couldn't afford to be late.

After breakfast, I followed Mitch to the day's ending point, a Dollar General in Mims. I hopped in his car, and he drove me to the restaurant where I left off. Along the way, Mitch talked about "having your must" – that thing (or person) that drives you, inspires you. Lola is Mitch's "must." She's the reason he fights Sturge-Weber syndrome and hosts charity events. Because of her and for her, he does all the great work he does.

I often reflect on this (though not in those exact terms) when I think about why I'm running down the coast and why I biked across America. Jenna is my "must." I wouldn't be doing any of this if not for her. In fact, I don't think I'd *be able to do it* if it wasn't for her. But there's something more, something I didn't anticipate; an unexpected benefit I'm sure Mitch can attest to. Doing these charity events has brought me real joy. To be able to help Jenna and so many others,

Al DeCesaris

and to see how it positively impacts their lives, has given me more than I could have ever imagined.

Not long after I got started, I saw an armadillo scurrying in the grass. Now, I'd seen armadillos before. During my bike ride, I must have pedaled past a hundred of them, but all of those were pancake-flat road kill. This was the first time I'd seen a live armadillo. Well, let me tell you, they're disgusting creatures. I could have done without that experience. However, it was better than coming upon a bobcat.

Other than that nasty critter, there wasn't anything of interest those first couple of hours. Route 1 was dominated by gas stations, convenience stores, and fast food joints. Not being able to run on A1A and take in the water views left me frustrated. Sad to say, it wasn't just for the day. I wouldn't be able to run on it for the next several because I was coming up on Kennedy Space Center and Cape Canaveral Air Force Station. Since A1A doesn't run through those areas, it was Route 1 in all its traffic light and drive-thru glory for the foreseeable future.

As I ran along wondering why NASA and the Air Force had to hog up all that prime oceanfront real estate, I tweaked my right calf. I wasn't sure how I did it, or the severity of it, but I thought it best to back off and walk for a while.

While I walked in frustration, I saw a car on the side of the road up ahead and people standing by it. I dismissed it at first, but then realized one of the people was Mitch. I soon learned that the other was Jo Ann

Bernau Haven, a friend of Mitch's and a real estate agent with his company, Tropical Realty. Mitch had brought her out to run with me. It was an awesome surprise and a huge pick-me-up.

Over the next couple of hours, I got to know Jo Ann and learned, aside from the fact that she's an amazing lady, she's also a very good runner. I had to dig deep to keep up with her. But it was great because it made the miles go by quicker and got my mind off my calf.

There was, however, a problem that surfaced during our time together. I'm not sure if it was the result of a glitch with Google Maps or just confusion on my part, but the number of miles I had to cover ended up being several more than I had originally thought. Every time I thought we were coming to the ending point, the road continued on. Under normal circumstances, this would have made me irate. But the way I looked at it, the farther I went today with a running partner, the fewer miles I'd have to go another day by myself. I don't know if Jo Ann was down with my theory, but there wasn't much we could do about it other than keep running. In the end, we ran 10 miles together, and I ran a total of 30.3 miles for the day, making it my longest day yet.

After driving to Mitch and Jeanette's house and getting cleaned up, I headed to UNO Pizzeria for the event. Along with Mitch, Jeanette and their family, a contingent from Tropical Realty were there, including my running partner Jo Ann and marketing director Amy Cevallos. Amy played a big role in promoting the event and made arrangements for me to run a leg of the upcoming Space Coast Marathon. I also met one of Jeanette's friends, Lana Saal, who might be my running partner tomorrow. Here's to hoping I convinced her to join me.

I didn't know what to the night would bring, but from the moment I arrived I could feel the love in the room. Everyone I met was so caring and supportive of our efforts to find a cure. It speaks volumes about how they feel about Mitch and Jeanette, and the love they have for Lola. These aren't casual bystanders; they're loyal and dedicated friends who stand with Mitch and Jeanette in the search for a cure and with the hope of bringing Lola and those like her a better life.

Day 83 (11/29/14): Mims, FL to Cocoa, FL [23.8 miles]

After two early mornings and a 30+ mile run yesterday, this morning I got to sleep in … and was loving life. Even better, I had more running partners lined up for today. Jeanette's son Michael accompanied me for the first couple of hours and Lana joined me later in the day. I suppose my sweet-talking worked on her.

Around 10:30am, Mitch and Jeanette dropped Michael and me off at the Dollar General in Mims. The original plan was to cover just shy of 24 miles, the majority of which would be on a busy, commercial stretch of Route 1. However, as we made our way to the starting point, Mitch determined that the last seven miles or so I could get off of Route 1 and onto a parallel residential road that runs along Indian River. I was super excited to hear that, even without knowing what Indian River looked like. It had to be better scenery than the strip-mall chaos of Route 1.

The weather today was fantastic. Temps were in the low 70s and billowy white clouds filled the sky providing occasional cover. Not bad for a late November day.

From the start, we set a quick pace, one that had me running faster than I normally do. It wasn't a conscious decision, mind you. It just seems to happen whenever I

Al DeCesaris

run with other people. Call it competitive spirit or what you will but having someone to run with pushes me (it's kind of like having a police car or bobcat behind you).

It was great to have company again, and we had fun ... at least I did. Michael lives in Chicago and was in town to visit his family for Thanksgiving weekend. I'm sure running with me wasn't how he anticipated spending his time. But as a fellow-uncle of a beautiful little girl with Sturge-Weber syndrome, he was more than eager to help the cause.

We met up with Mitch and Jeanette in Titusville at a location on the side of the road with sweeping views of Indian River. Across the river is NASA's Kennedy Space Center, the United States' preeminent center for space exploration where space flights have launched since the 1960s. Talk about a fantastic backdrop for a photo. Jeanette made sure to get a nice one of Michael and me to commemorate the "uncles' run."

Mitch, Jeanette, and Michael then headed out, and I continued on. Over the next several hours, I ran down Route 1. And every so often, I caught a glimpse of Indian River, which was a nice incentive and helped pass the time. Even better, this stretch of Route 1 had both a wide shoulder and a sidewalk most of the way. This allowed me to focus on my form to protect my right calf (which, I'm happy to report, held up well today).

In the early afternoon, I came to the residential road Mitch had mentioned. It's a narrow road with beautiful homes, majestic oaks, stately palms, and spectacular

Running The Coast For A Cure

water views. I'd run a lot of scenic roads during this journey, but few as gorgeous as this one.

A few miles along, Mitch and Jeanette pulled up with running partner number two, Lana Saal. She had a smile on her face and looked ready to roll. After pictures (with scenery like that we couldn't pass up the opportunity to get a few pics), we were off and running. Like I said before, I enjoy having company when I run, and it definitely pushes me. But I had trouble keeping up with Lana and talking. Either she didn't get the memo – if you can't carry a conversation while running, you're running too fast – or she did get it and that's why she was running as fast as she did. All kidding aside, we had a great time together (even if it was a struggle for me).

As we neared Cocoa Village, the historic tree-lined shopping district where we were to end the run, Mitch and Jeanette pulled up again. This time with high school track star Dominique Coriell. You think it was tough keeping up with Lana, try keeping pace with a teenage track star ... not a chance. The only positive was we didn't have far to go. Otherwise, I would have been in all kinds of trouble.

When we arrived in Cocoa Village and ran the last couple of blocks to the day's ending point, people in the street were cheering us on. Now, I don't know if Mitch and Jeanette started that up, but it was a very cool way to finish the run.

After saying my goodbyes to my running partners and new friends, Lana and Dominique, I got into Mitch's car and we headed back to the house for a relaxing

Al DeCesaris

evening. Because tomorrow is the Space Coast Marathon, it was an early night for me. Before nodding off to sleep, I reflected on how much Mitch and Jeanette, and their friends and family, have done for me. They have gone out of their way to make me feel welcomed and have done everything in their power to help me on my journey. Connecting with them, being in their care, having their support … is a real blessing.

Day 84 (11/30/14): Cocoa, FL to Palm Bay, FL [25.6 miles]

Race Day! That's right, today was the Space Coast Marathon in Cocoa. Props to Amy at Tropical Realty for making arrangements so I could run a portion of it. And props to Ida for making sure yesterday's ending point was right at the race's starting line, and the miles I'd run during the race were along my route.

To be there in time for the 6am start, I had to drag myself out of bed at four o'clock. As you know, getting up early isn't my thing, especially at an obnoxiously early hour like that, but I didn't want to miss out on this. The race was supposed to be a blast, and the course went along Indian River. There was *no way* I was passing that up.

The Space Coast Marathon is actually both a full and half marathon. The interesting thing about it, at least to me, is that it has a "space" theme celebrating the "Space Coast," the region around Kennedy Space Center and Cape Canaveral Air Force Station. As an aside, the region even has the area code 321 in recognition of the 3-2-1 countdown before a liftoff. Of course, all of this enthusiasm is coming from a guy who wanted to go to "Space Camp" as a kid. Come on, don't

Al DeCesaris

laugh. If you had seen the movie *Space Camp* when you were 13, you'd have nagged your parents to go too.

Mitch dropped me off a half hour before the start, giving me time to scope things out, and check out all the crazy costumes people were wearing. There were astronauts, aliens, Star Wars and Star Trek characters, among others. Even the race volunteers were dressed up, in NASA uniforms. Adding to the excitement, music blared, and people were bouncing around like it was a dance party. Whether you were wearing a Darth Vader costume or a hydration pack like yours truly, there was no way not to get caught up in the festive atmosphere.

As I made my way through the crowds to the starting line, I got more and more excited. Yet, I couldn't let my excitement get the best of me. Unlike everyone else, I'll have to run roughly a marathon again tomorrow, and the day after that ... and again ... and again. So, I reminded myself to maintain *my* pace and decided to wait until all the runners got going before I began the race.

Just before 6am, a Jumbotron at the starting line displayed a Space Shuttle on the launch pad, and a booming voice initiated the countdown. When the voice reached "3-2-1 liftoff," a deafening roar erupted, and the Shuttle launched into the sky. I've never seen a Space Shuttle launch in person, but this was pretty darn cool.

With several thousand participants, it took close to 10 minutes for all the runners to cross the starting line. Once I saw the last of them cross, I began my "Space Coast Marathon" (actually, my run today was 25.6 miles, but close enough). The good thing about starting in last

316

Running The Coast For A Cure

place was I couldn't finish the race any worse than I started it. Jokes aside, I was only running the portion of the course that coincided with my route, which was about six miles.

Around the corner from Cocoa Village, the course turned onto a road that ran along Indian River with spectacular views like the ones I saw yesterday. Yet, things got even better when the sun began its ascent. As runners dashed down the course in a throng, I trotted along by myself watching the rising sun transform the sky from blue to pink to orange and yellow, while infusing the clouds with morning light and casting brilliant hues on the water.

After stopping a handful of times to take pictures, I decided I couldn't take being in last place any longer. I picked up the pace, and soon caught up with the pack. I then started passing people, first the walkers then the slower runners. The more people I passed, the faster I found myself running. Even though I knew better, before long I was running like I was trying to win the race.

The six-mile mark came before I knew it. With disappointment, I peeled off of the course and headed toward the road I needed to take. The race volunteers working that area must have thought I was confused because they tried to direct me back onto the course. I assured them it was no mistake. Route 1 was just ahead, and I needed to get back to the regularly scheduled program.

It was Route 1 the rest of the way ... it was also significant back pain (below my right shoulder) the rest of the way. The problem with this injury (or whatever it is), it flares up time and again without warning. Even though it has never gotten so bad that I've needed to take time off, when it does rear its ugly head, it hurts like a son of a gun.

To my surprise and appreciation, as I ran (and battled the pain) I was afforded more breathtaking views. For long stretches, Route 1 ran right along Indian River, with nothing other than palm trees between me and the water. Despite the views, the warm weather and Florida sun were again getting the best of me. I ended up going through all my water toward the end of the day, and dehydration became a concern.

A little before noon, I reached the day's ending point, a motel in Palm Bay. While I waited for Mitch and Jeanette to pick me up, I went next door to a convenience store for Gatorade. As I downed the first bottle (in a matter of seconds) and cracked open the second, I wondered how the Marathon racers had faired. Were they chugging Gatorades trying to recover? More likely, they were celebrating their achievement with their feet kicked up and a cocktail in hand. I, on the other hand, had to do this again tomorrow and….

Still, I'll soon be doing some celebrating of my own. Tomorrow will be the first day of December and, if I stick to my schedule, I only have nine more days to go before I reach Key Largo. It's single digits from here on out. Let the countdown begin. How fitting that the countdown should begin on the Space Coast.

Day 85 (12/1/14): Palm Bay, FL to Vero Beach, FL [25.6 miles]

According to the schedule Ida made for me, after today's 25+ mile run I'd be in Vero Beach. The city is situated in Indian River County well south of where Mitch and Jeanette live. So, after four great days with the Ribaks, it was time to move on.

After breakfast, I packed my things and said goodbye to Jeanette. It was wonderful to get to know her better and spend time with her and her family. She's an amazing person, and Lola is one lucky little girl to have Jeanette as her grandma.

Mitch followed me to the day's ending point in Vero Beach, the Springhill Suites hotel where I'm staying for the night (thanks to Will Futch for booking yet another room for me). Mitch then drove me back to the motel in Palm Bay where I left off yesterday.

As we said our goodbyes, I thought about everything he and Jeanette have done for me: the meals, the rides, the running partners. I also reflected on the love they have for Lola. I know to most, saying that grandparents love their grandchild seems like an overstatement of the obvious. But these aren't your typical grandparents, and their love for Lola is far from ordinary. Mitch and Jeanette have made their granddaughter's well-being

Al DeCesaris

their number one priority. They have done (and continue to do) everything they can to help her overcome her challenges and live a healthier and happier life. Not only are they heroes in her eyes, they're heroes in mine.

Around 10:30am, I started my run. Right off the bat, I had spectacular views of Indian River. Like yesterday, Route 1 ran along the water and had a wide shoulder where I could run without worry and take in the riverscape. It wasn't just for a few miles. It was several hours of sundrenched waters, palm trees, and sailboats. To think, just a few days ago I was whining about having to leave A1A. Next time, I'll wait before passing judgment.

A little later, a guy driving by blew the horn and gave me a thumbs-up. It had been a while since I'd received encouragement from a stranger like that. In fact, it had been a while since I'd had any interactions with drivers. I think the last time I did, it was that hillbilly in the pickup truck who ran me off the road … or maybe it was that evil old woman who tried to run me over. All the thumbs-ups in the world won't get me over that.

Evidently, it wasn't just hillbillies and evil old women who had it out for me. As I was running along, a guy on a bicycle rode up beside me and attempted to elbow me as he passed. *What the heck?!?* I proceeded to give him a piece of my mind. Well, I must have said something he didn't like – perhaps it was where I told him he could go – because he hit the brakes and turned toward me with a menacing look in his eyes. At that point, this thing could have gone down a number of different ways, most of which wouldn't have been good for me or the nut job

Running The Coast For A Cure

on the bike. I knew I had to get away from him and fast. So, with mace at the ready, I ran past him without making eye contact and without saying a word. When he got going again and pedaled past me, there were no flying elbows this time. I suppose my effort to appear "disinterested" worked. I only wish it worked on crazy canines as well.

Not long after, I reached the city of Sebastian. There, Route 1 tracked away from the river and took me through a commercial area. It wasn't the most picturesque scenery, but after the gorgeous run I just had, I couldn't complain.

A little while later, it started to rain. As you know, running in the rain isn't my favorite thing, so I took cover under the awning of a nearby shopping center and waited it out. It didn't last long, but it put me on notice that in Florida rain can come without warning. This notion was reinforced toward the end of the day when out of nowhere it started pouring. This time there were no buildings nearby, so I huddled under some trees until it passed. It was a pain in the tail, but hey, it's Florida.

About a mile before reaching the day's ending point, some jerk in a pickup truck revved his engine right as I ran by, blowing exhaust in my face. You might think it was an accident, but I assure you it wasn't. The grin on the guy's face said it all. Of course, I let him know what I thought about it by flipping him the bird. I'll admit, it wasn't the most mature way to handle the situation. But cut me some slack. This was the second time today someone messed with me.

Al DeCesaris

It was a disappointing end to the day. Yet, I've been on the road long enough to know things like this happen. In a way, it's like the Florida rain; it comes out of nowhere, often when you least expect it. It's the positive stuff, the support of friends like Mitch and Jeanette, the encouragement of random strangers giving a thumbs up, that pulls me through. It's that positivity that helps me continue on and keeps me running.

Day 86 (12/2/14): Vero Beach, FL to Fort Pierce, FL [23 miles]

Around 10:30am, I packed my things and got ready for the day, which was to be a wet one according the weather forecast. As you can imagine, I wasn't eager to get out there and slosh around in the rain. Still, I had a schedule to follow and miles to cover. I donned my poncho and set out with little enthusiasm.

The plan was to run 23 miles to the city of Fort Pierce where I'd meet up with my fraternity brother, Pat Cunnane. He was to drive me back to the hotel so I could get my car. I'd then follow him to his house in Palm City where I'm staying tonight and tomorrow night. Have I mentioned how much easier things would be if I had a dedicated driver? I guess I should just be thankful that Pat had volunteered to help. I could be scrambling around trying to find a ride back to my car … or worse, hitchhiking. I still can't believe I actually did that.

From the hotel, I followed Indian River Boulevard, which runs parallel to Route 1 through a suburban area. Though the rain came down steadily, the temperature was in the mid 70s, making the run tolerable (even by my standards). About six miles in, the road connected with Route 1. This stretch of the familiar highway has three lanes going in each direction with a multitude of businesses along the roadway. I dislike busy commercial roads as much as I do sleepy rural ones, but there was a sidewalk there, which kept me a safe distance from speeding vehicles and splashing water.

Speaking of rural roads, less than an hour later, Google Maps led me onto Old Dixie Highway; a narrow, shoulder-less road with little to see other than oaks, palms, and dense vegetation. It seemed 100 miles from civilization. Meanwhile, Route 1 was only a quarter of a mile to my right and the Intercoastal a half mile to my left.

Not far into it, the rain tapered off, and my upper right back started to hurt; one problem replaced another. Though it wasn't just today, my back has been acting up the past several days. Of all the injuries I've had over the past three months, who'd have thought an upper back injury would be the one I couldn't shake?

As I struggled along, my thoughts shifted to what lay ahead. After today's run, weather permitting and barring any unforeseen problems, my journey would be down to its last seven days. During that time, I'll be staying with a couple of old friends and the parents of another, meeting up with an elementary school classmate, reconnecting with my parents, and meeting two children who have Sturge-Weber syndrome. I'm super excited about it all ... and, of course, about finishing the run. Yet, what I'm really looking forward to is meeting these two children and their families. Up until now, I haven't had much interaction of this kind, so to be able to meet

Running The Coast For A Cure

two families affected by Sturge-Weber syndrome in the final week of my run was fortuitous and fantastic.

In the afternoon, Old Dixie Highway merged with Route 1 and I found myself in a busy and rather sketchy section of Fort Pierce. I'm not sure if it was my surroundings, my ailing back or just plain old fatigue, but all at once I ran out of steam. The last hour and half of the day was a real struggle.

As I battled through it, I passed a store with a mannequin sitting out front with a bizarre-looking mask over its face. I must have swung my head around a half dozen times trying to figure out what the heck it was. It looked like the face of a haggard man with exaggerated features and a shock of curly black hair. It was one of the strangest things I've seen.

About a half hour later, I reached the shopping center in Fort Pierce, which was the day's ending point. When I stepped into the parking lot, I was greeted by the masked mannequin, who was none other than my fraternity brother Pat in a Halloween mask. I should have known. In college, Pat was notorious for pranks like that. Just to give you an idea of what I'm talking about, he once put poop in another fraternity brother's soap dish. Imagine waking up in the morning, jumping in the shower, and finding that little surprise when you reached for the soap. It had been a while since I'd seen him, but obviously he was still up to his old tricks.

That evening, we were treated to a delicious pasta dinner compliments of Pat's fiancé Susan. Also joining us was Joe, one of Pat's childhood friends from

Pennsylvania who is coincidentally his current neighbor. As they drank wine and I ate seconds (and thirds), I told them about Jenna and the cause. They couldn't have been more supportive and encouraging. I had always known Pat to be a kindhearted person, so it came as no surprise that he and those closest to him would welcome me as they had. Still, I was keeping my eyes open while I was there … and checking the soap dish before I put my hands in it.

Day 87 (12/3/14): Fort Pierce, FL to Hobe Sound, FL [25.6 miles]

Around 9:45am, Pat (sans the mask) dropped me off at the shopping center in Fort Pierce where I left off. I'm happy to report, I received nothing other than encouragement from him this morning. Keep in mind, I still have another night at his house, so I'm not in the clear just yet.

My plan for the day was to cover 25.6 miles, all of which would be on Route 1. Pat would pick me up at my ending point, a convenience store in Hobe Sound. In the evening, I was to meet Annie Vititoe and her four-year-old daughter Arayah, who has Sturge-Weber syndrome. Although I really looked forward to meeting them, I could have done without another day on Route 1.

Like yesterday, Route 1 had multiple lanes going in each direction, all congested with traffic. Even though it had a sidewalk to run on, it was hard to get into a rhythm because I had to keep stopping at intersections and shopping center entranceways. I must admit, there was a quiet road running along Indian River that I could have taken. The "scenic route," however, would have added about three and a half miles to the day's run. As you know, I love my water views, but the way I felt

Al DeCesaris

today, running extra miles (even one extra) wasn't happening.

You would think, after a good night's sleep and a hearty breakfast, I'd have lots of energy. Yet, that wasn't the case. Within the first couple of hours, I was fatigued. Was it the heat? The temperature *was* about 80 degrees, though I'd run in warm weather countless times before. It *had* to be more than that. Perhaps the humidity was affecting me....

By the time I reached the St. Lucie River, which was about 12 miles in, I was sweating my tail off and utterly exhausted. Before crossing the bridge, I stopped at a convenience store for a couple of cold drinks. I sat in the shade out front of the store for some time trying to recover. If my condition was the result of the heat and humidity, I could only imagine how difficult things would have been if I'd done this run during the summer months. It was December for crying out loud!

Once I got going again, I took to the bridge and enjoyed fantastic views of the river and the boats (and yachts) in its waters. This infused some life into me ... or maybe it was the two energy drinks I'd just gulped down and all their sugary goodness. Either way, when I reached Stuart, on the other side of the bridge, I felt somewhat better.

The remainder of the way, Route 1 was teeming with commercial development and congestion. During the last few hours, I also had to deal with that nagging back pain again. Sadly, those five sugar-high, pain-free minutes on the bridge were as good as things got today.

Running The Coast For A Cure

A couple of miles before the end of the run, Pat showed up with water and to see how I was doing. No, he wasn't wearing a mask and there weren't any pranks involved. He just wanted to make sure I was alright. It meant a lot to me and gave me a boost. A little later, I met up with Pat again when I reached the convenience store in Hobe Sound, which was the day's ending point.

When we got back to his house, I jumped in the shower and was relieved to find a clean bar of soap and no hidden surprises. Afterward, I iced my legs and guzzled ice water as I tried to recoup my strength. It had been a long, hot day, and I was completely wiped out.

Later that evening, I went to a local Panera Bread to meet Annie and Arayah. Even though we had never met, as soon as we did, we were fast friends. Annie was so warm and kind and Arayah was adorable and sweet. Her condition is similar to Jenna's in that she has a port-wine birthmark on her face and has suffered severe seizures, leaving her with learning disabilities. Despite those difficulties and the daily challenges associated with Sturge-Weber syndrome, Arayah attends special needs pre-K at the local public school and is one of the more advanced students in her class.

As we ate dinner, I told Annie about my run and colored pictures with Arayah. It was wonderful to spend time with them and get to know them. Experiences like this make the long, difficult, and hot days on the road worthwhile. For me, interactions with these incredible individuals are what it's all about.

Day 88 (12/4/14): Hobe Sound, FL to West Palm Beach, FL [26 miles]

I woke up in the middle of the night with the room spinning. *What's going on?* I questioned as a wave of nausea overcame me. I stumbled into the bathroom and grabbed the toilet bowl. Did I have the flu? … food poisoning? … was it the result of dehydration? I hovered over the toilet, waiting…. After some time, the feeling subsided and I was able to return to bed. Still, something wasn't right, and it had me very concerned.

In the morning, I woke up feeling better. This came as a real surprise. I had figured I'd be sick in bed all day. Well, if the worst of it (whatever it was) was behind me, I wanted to get my miles in, or at least try. As planned, Pat and Susan left for work before I got up. So, after I packed my things and loaded up my car, their friend Joe followed me to the day's ending point. He and Susan had contacts at a TV station in West Palm Beach and were trying to arrange a news interview for me. Based on that (and because their contacts said I could leave my car at the station), I made the station my ending point. After parking my car in their lot, Joe drove me to the convenience store in Hobe Sound where I left off.

When I started, it was raining. Yet, I wasn't about to let a little rain (or the sauna-like poncho I was wearing) dampen my spirits. A bunch of good things were working for me today: I had the possibility of a TV news interview, I'd be returning to A1A and, most important, I'd be running as opposed to leaning over a toilet.

Early on, the commercial development along Route 1 fell away and I came to an area with grassy dunes to my left and unspoiled parkland to my right. At various points, I had fantastic views of Indian River and the gorgeous and renowned Jupiter Island beyond it. Not a bad way to start the run … and 45 minutes later, the rain let up, making things even better.

Not long after, I ran past the Jupiter Inlet Lighthouse and over Loxahatchee River. I then turned onto A1A and began an amazing run through Jupiter and Juno Beach. In these areas, A1A runs right along the ocean. The views were off the charts. The excitement of it all increased my pace. As well as I was moving, it was hard to believe I'd felt as sick as I had last night.

When I think about situations like last night and all the adversity I've faced during this run, I recognize how fortunate I've been. Over the past three months, I've run almost every day and haven't needed to take more than one day off at a time. Factoring in the number of miles I've covered and the injuries I've sustained, it's remarkable I'm still standing, much less in the home-stretch. It's more than good fortune, I realize. The little girl in my heart gives me determination, and the Man upstairs gives me strength. As a result, this seemingly impossible task has become possible.

Running The Coast For A Cure

In the early afternoon, I merged back onto Route 1 and found myself amid commercial development and congestion. There wasn't much to see other than strip malls, though it was a nice area, and there was a sidewalk to keep me safe. However, as I got closer to West Palm Beach, my surroundings deteriorated. Before long, it became rundown and dicey. I hadn't expected this. Though, I figured it was just a small pocket and when I reached West Palm things would improve. Sad to say, when I entered the city and turned onto the back roads that led to the TV station, things got worse. It was one of the shadiest neighborhoods I'd run through.

Although I hadn't received confirmation of the interview, I was told to be at the station at 5:30pm and that they'd try to have a reporter there. Running 26 miles isn't easy under normal circumstances, but not feeling 100% and having to be there at a specific time made things challenging. The last few miles were tough, and I had to run hard to reach the station in time … and to get through that shady neighborhood safe.

Lucky for me, I succeeded on both accounts. When I arrived at the station, I was happy to see a reporter setting up out front. I introduced myself and told him I needed a couple of minutes to catch my breath. I then went over to my car, sucked down a bottle of water and toweled myself dry … and fixed my hair (I had to look good for the TV camera).

When I walked back, the reporter was interviewing someone else. I was confused, but assumed I'd be next and waited for them to finish. However, when they were done, the reporter started packing up his gear. I was then told by one of the producers that they didn't have anyone from the appropriate department available to interview me. I was baffled (why the heck couldn't this reporter do it?!?) as well as irritated and embarrassed. I had rolled up to that guy like I was "the man." Meanwhile, he didn't have a clue who I was and probably thought I was nuts. Considering the fact that I ran through one of the most dangerous neighborhoods to get there in time, I just might be.

The sting of it wore off when I got to the home of Fran and Charlie Cannone, who had offered to host me for a couple of nights. (They're the parents of Mike, one of my best friends from college.) It had been years since I had seen them. Yet, when I arrived, they welcomed me with open arms. That evening, they took me to dinner at 5Ocean in Delray Beach, where their son Brian and his wife Dawn work. The food and the company were great, and we had a wonderful evening together.

As much as I've complained about not having a dedicated driver, this run wouldn't be as much fun, as interesting, or as rewarding if one person handled all the driving duties. I would have missed out on meeting and spending time with so many awesome people. In retrospect, despite the stress and anxiety of not having a dedicated driver, I couldn't be happier with the way things have worked out.

Day 89 (12/5/14): West Palm Beach, FL to Boca Raton, FL [26.5 miles]

After breakfast, I followed Mrs. Cannone to the Flashback Diner in Boca Raton, the day's ending point. I parked my car in their lot, and she drove me back to the TV station where I left off yesterday.

From the moment I started, I could tell that today's run was going to be an uphill battle. Of course, not literally, there aren't any hills around these parts. Rather, I was dead tired and felt weak. Was I coming down with something? Most likely, it was dehydration. No doubt, the humidity in Florida has worked me over since I arrived. And it seems the farther south I go, the worse it gets.

Not far along, I came to a seedy and neglected neighborhood similar to the one I ran through yesterday. It wasn't how I wanted to start the day, but at least I didn't get any threatening looks. Still, I made sure not to linger. Despite my lack of energy, I got clear of the neighborhood rather quickly. Nothing like fear to motivate you.

Once I reached a safer part of the city, I settled into what would become my "record-setting" pace, which was something between a sluggish jog and a heavy-

Al DeCesaris

footed walk. As pathetic as it was, it was the best I could do.

About an hour in, I spotted a McDonald's and decided to take a break and get something to eat. As I devoured fries and guzzled a Powerade (and wallowed in the air-conditioning), I wondered if my exhaustion was indeed the result of dehydration. The plan for the day was to run roughly 25 miles. Was trying to cover such a distance in heat and humidity in my condition a mistake? Would it lead to more problems?

After the break, I set back out, hopeful the rest and sustenance would give me an upsurge. However, it didn't give me much of anything, nor did the scenery. The next hour took me through a monotonous commercial area, which coupled with the heat and my fatigue, made me feel like I wasn't making any progress. I needed a change of scenery and something positive to focus on. Even though I knew getting onto A1A would add extra mileage, I abandoned Google Maps' walking route and crossed the Intercoastal.

I then turned onto A1A and made my way through the seaside town of Manalapan. There, I was treated to gorgeous views of both the Intercoastal and the ocean. It was just what the doctor ordered.

About three miles down A1A, I crossed Boynton Inlet and entered Ocean Ridge. The road then moved away from the beach just enough for me to lose sight of it. However, A1A through this area did have plenty to see – there were impressive condominium communities, spectacular oceanfront homes, and an assortment of palm trees and landscaped vegetation.

A little farther along, I came to the mobile home community, Briny Breezes. Around that point I started to feel very lethargic and was all but convinced I was dehydrated. So, I stopped at a market for something to drink and bought a coconut water, which is supposed to be even better for hydration than my go-to sports drinks. I also had the guy at the deli counter set me up with a shot of pickle juice. It sounds crazy, but I heard pickle juice works wonders on dehydration. Who knows if there's any truth to that…. Nevertheless, it couldn't hurt to give it a try.

Later that afternoon, I passed through Delray Beach, a cool seaside city with lots of shops, galleries, restaurants, and bars. In the heart of the city, A1A runs along a fantastic public beach. However, the sky soon grew dark and minutes later I was hunkered down under a tree, waiting out a torrential downpour (that's break #3 for those keeping track).

About a mile farther down the road, I turned onto Linton Boulevard and headed toward the Intercoastal. As I was making my way across the bridge, by chance Mr. Cannone drove by. Around that time, the coconut-pickle cocktail must have worn off because I was plodding along at a sloth-like pace with my head hanging low. Mr. Cannone probably wondered if I was going to make it. I was starting to wonder myself.

Break #4 came toward the end of the day. This one also was the result of hard rain. You know Florida, the rain comes and goes. And as quickly as it came, it went. I only wish the humidity went with it.

Around 5pm, I reached the Flashback Diner, completing my "record setting" day … though it wasn't record-setting because it was so fast. Today was my longest day (time-wise) of the entire run, seven and a half hours in all. I suppose that's what happens when you alternate between a super-slow jog and an even slower walk and take four breaks.

Despite the amount of time it took and considering how bad I felt, I'm proud I got my miles in, all 26.5 of them. My efforts today brought to mind the words of Confucius, "it does not matter how slowly you go as long as you do not stop."

Day 90 (12/6/14): Boca Raton, FL to Dania Beach, FL [26 miles]

It was another morning of goodbyes. My stay with the Cannones had been great, but it was time again to move on. My whirlwind tour was taking me to Ft. Lauderdale and the home of Shawn Vernon.

When I got to Shawn's apartment, he greeted me with enthusiasm. We then went to a local diner for breakfast. As we chatted, I stuffed my face and guzzled glass after glass of water. In light of yesterday's difficulties, I wanted to make sure I was properly hydrated and had lots of carbs to burn.

When we got back to his place, I readied myself for the day while Shawn finalized plans with his friend Sandy to drop us off and pick us up. Shawn offered to ride his bicycle alongside me and take photos and shoot video of me as I covered my miles. As many photos as I have of the run, I have few of me actually running. I don't think Shawn knew what he was getting himself into, but I was thrilled to have him join me.

Once his bike was loaded into the trunk of my car, we drove to Lauderdale-By-The-Sea to pick up Sandy. We then headed to the Flashback Diner in Boca Raton where I left off. After turning my car over to Sandy, we started down Route 1, me on foot, Shawn on wheels.

Al DeCesaris

A few minutes in, we came to a small park with a Christmas tree in the center of a semicircle of Palm trees. It was funny to see a Christmas tree in 80-degree weather with the sun shining bright overhead. For me, the Christmas season is typically accompanied by cold weather and the occasional snowman. I guess they don't get many white Christmases in South Florida. Though I'll take the sunshine over the snow any day.

We turned east onto Palmetto Park Road, went over the Intercoastal, and got onto A1A. This stretch of the state road runs between the Intercoastal and high-rise condo complexes overlooking the ocean. A mile farther, we crossed a bridge over Boca Raton Inlet, affording us great views of both the Intercoastal and the inlet.

Boca Raton then gave way to the city of Deerfield Beach. The city's public beach and fishing pier provided a scenic backdrop for my run (and my photos too). There was lots of people-watching to be had as well. There's nothing like sun, surf, and sand – and bikinis – to put a little spring in your step.

Next up was Hillsboro Beach. As we made our way through town, I ran and Shawn pedaled along "Millionaires' Mile." Oddly enough, it's about *three* miles long. I later learned the name refers to all the mansions lining the road (presumably, owned by millionaires), not its length. At least they got one part of the name right.

We then came to Hillsboro Inlet. From the bridge that spans the inlet, we had great views of the black-and-white Hillsboro Lighthouse and the Atlantic Ocean. I've

Running The Coast For A Cure

seen several lighthouses during my journey, but this one, with its iron pyramidal shape, was unlike any other.

On the far side of the inlet was Pompano Beach. This seaside city is very different from Hillsboro in that it has a mixture of homes, condo complexes, and hotels. Not far down, we left A1A for a spell to run along the city's public beach – a scenic half-mile-stretch with sidewalks and Palm trees running along manicured-grassy areas and a wide sandy beach.

Our next stop on the ocean-side tour was Lauderdale-by-Sea. As we made our way through town, Shawn peeled off to take a break at Sandy's place. There were no breaks for me, however. I had more miles to cover and no time to waste. So, while my good buddy lounged in the A/C with a cold drink in hand, I kept trucking down A1A in the Florida heat and humidity.

Shawn caught up with me about an hour later as I was getting into Ft. Lauderdale. Unlike the other areas I'd run through today, Ft. Lauderdale is a big city. We followed A1A as it ran between a gorgeous public beach and a promenade with high-end boutiques, restaurants, and hotels. It's a very cool area and worth a visit ... when you're not running all day and dripping with sweat.

A1A then turned inland to get around the city's port. According to Google Maps, a mile ahead A1A merges with Route 1. As we neared the intersection where the roads meet, Shawn made a left turn just as an oncoming van came barreling down the road. At the last second, the van slammed on the brakes and Shawn veered out of the way, narrowly avoiding getting hit. Throughout this

Al DeCesaris

journey, the good Lord has been looking out for me and keeping me safe. It seems He is looking out for Shawn as well.

After we got our heart-rates down, we continued on and soon were back on Route 1. However, this stretch of Route 1 prohibits pedestrians. So, we had to take a convoluted route adding about a mile to the day's run. It wasn't the end of the world, especially in light of what had just transpired, but it was irritating nonetheless. The "detour" cost time and landed us on a dimly-lit road after sundown. I had to run my tail off to get back to Route 1 before visibility diminished. Luckily, we reached the sidewalk and streetlights of Route 1 without running into any problems … or speeding vans.

Shawn stopped at a gas station on Route 1 where he met Sandy. While they loaded his bike into my car, I ran the last half mile to the day's ending point (the intersection of Route 1 and Dania Beach Boulevard) and closed out the day's 26-mile run brimming with energy. As strong as I finished, it was hard to believe I felt as bad as I had yesterday. It was even harder to believe I've been on the road for 90 days and am now in the final days of this epic journey. In light of where I started physically, the adversity I've faced, and the injuries I've sustained, I know without a doubt the good Lord is looking out for me and is the author of my success.

Day 91 (12/7/14): Dania Beach, FL to Miami, FL [26.3 miles]

It was to be another busy day. The plan was to run a marathon from Dania Beach through a half dozen beach towns to the city of Miami. After my run, I'd reconnect with my parents, who flew in today. We'd then head to South Beach for a celebratory dinner with Bari and Corey Clark and their son Cole, who has Sturge-Weber syndrome. Also joining us would be Shawn and Dawn Debus, one of my elementary school classmates.

After breakfast, Shawn dropped me off at yesterday's ending point. He wouldn't be joining me today. I think the close encounter with the speeding van had been enough "excitement" for him. I couldn't blame him. He did come *very* close to getting run over. Plus, he hosted me last night, was driving me today, and spent all day yesterday with me taking photos and shooting video. I'd say he has done more than his fair share for the cause.

The first hour of the run took me through Dania Beach and into Hollywood. I then crossed the Intercoastal into Hallandale Beach and got onto A1A. This section of A1A has high-rise buildings lining both sides of the road. With the exception of Palm trees throughout the area, it appeared more like a bustling city than a laid-back seaside community. However, that

Al DeCesaris

imposing urban feel vanished the second I crossed the county line, leaving Broward and entering Miami-Dade County.

The first whistle stop was Golden Beach, a small upscale town made up primarily of stately homes. Even though most of them were hidden behind tall hedges and gated walls (apparently these well-to-do folks like their privacy), the ones I did see were impressive.

Just beyond Golden Beach was Sunny Isles Beach, a resort city with condos, hotels, restaurants, and shops. Because of all the waterfront complexes, I had no views of the ocean and just a scant few of the Intercoastal. Regardless, the sun was shining, and I felt great. Looking forward to the evenings' festivities sure helped. And knowing that I'd be done in a couple of days was an added bonus.

As you can imagine, I'm ecstatic about finishing up. Still, I don't think it has sunk in yet. I've been out on the road for so long this has become my norm. It's hard to imagine waking up in a few days and not having to run.

As I made my way farther, A1A took me through Haulover Park, a 99-acre public recreation area situated along both the Intercoastal and the ocean. At that point, I got onto a pedestrian path, Atlantic Way, which runs alongside the ocean. Along that stretch, there's a clothing optional beach. Though I'm disappointed to report, I didn't see anything more – or less – than usual.

I crossed Baker's Haulover Inlet and had a brief stay (er … run) in Bal Harbour before entering Surfside. I then returned to Atlantic Way and followed the ocean-side path into world-famous Miami Beach. From the path, I enjoyed phenomenal views of the white sand beach and turquoise blue ocean.

After a few blissful miles, the path ended, and I returned to A1A (known in this area as Collins Avenue). Although I would have preferred to continue running along the ocean, the sights from the road were captivating. Posh hotels of colorful Art Deco architecture, islets abounding with mansions, and waterways filled with yachts, made this leg of the run extremely entertaining. My only disappointment was, Google Maps had me heading west toward the Intercoastal (which in this area is called Biscayne Bay) before I got to South Beach, though I would get to see the popular tourist destination this evening.

I followed Venetian Way and its series of manmade islets over Biscayne Bay. As I island hopped across the water, I got stuck at two different drawbridges and had to wait for quite some time as huge boats passed. (There was a lot of "yacht traffic" today.) I can't gripe though, I had breathtaking views of Biscayne Bay and the Miami skyline.

I then turned onto Route 1 and continued south through downtown Miami. This stretch of road took me past the Adrienne Arsht Center for the Performing Arts, the Pérez Art Museum, and the American Airlines Arena, home of the NBA's Miami Heat. Soon after, I reached the day's ending point, a hotel on Route 1. Shawn met me there and we went to meet my parents.

Al DeCesaris

It meant the world to me that they had flown down to Florida to see me finish the run. Chauffeured rides and free meals the next couple of days wouldn't hurt either. All kidding aside, I am very fortunate to have such loving and supportive parents. After a heartfelt reunion, we headed to Monty's in South Beach for dinner.

Monty's is a lively restaurant in the fun and vibrant neighborhood of South Beach. Although I couldn't partake in the celebratory drinking and dancing (it's water and rest for a couple more days), I had a blast just the same. An amazing group of family and friends had come out to celebrate my journey and support the cause, including my parents, Shawn, Dawn and her friend Richard, along with Bari, Corey, and Cole Clark.

It was also special in that I got to spend time with three-year-old Cole. Despite his struggles with seizures, Cole is handsome and happy little guy, who has been hitting all of his developmental milestones. Meeting another Sturge-Weber child who will benefit from the awareness and funds we're raising for research, makes the final days of the run all the more meaningful.

Day 92 (12/8/14): Miami, FL to Homestead, FL [25.8 miles]

Aside from my normal sore and stiff legs, I woke with tempered enthusiasm. It was the last day before the last day, and even though I still had two full days and 50 miles of running ahead of me, I felt like I was just about there. Still, I needed to stay focused and keep to my routine, which included, among other things, a huge breakfast, lots of water, and my morning cup of joe.

After I did some serious damage at the hotel's breakfast buffet and went through my pre-run checklist, my parents dropped me off at the location in Miami where I left off yesterday. Today I was to run almost another full marathon from Miami to Homestead, ending my day at the Floridian Hotel where I'm staying tonight.

At the start, Google Maps directed me off of Route 1 and into the city's oldest continuously occupied neighborhood, Coconut Grove. For the first few miles, I ran parallel to Biscayne Bay, though I didn't get a good look at it until I reached Myers Bayside Park. There, I enjoyed postcard worthy views of the sundrenched waters and a fleet of sailboats just offshore. Google Maps then guided me west through the heart of the Grove and past myriad restaurants, bars, and boutiques. It's a cool area with an artsy and eclectic vibe.

Al DeCesaris

About a mile farther, I crossed into Coral Gables and got back onto Route 1. It was a busy and hectic stretch of road. It seemed every five seconds I was forced to stop so a car could turn down a side street or into a parking lot. Not that I hadn't run plenty of miles like that over the past few months, but after the scenic and relatively relaxing runs I've enjoyed as of late, this was really annoying.

Soon after, I came to the University of Miami, home of the Hurricanes. As I ran past it, I hoped to see a bit of the campus. Yet, to my disappointment, I didn't see much of anything other than signs for the university. Apparently, "The U" (as it's referred to by its students and alumni) was not to be part of my East Coast running tour.

Not long after, my right upper back started bothering me. It had been several days since I had any problems with it. I thought I might finish the run without having to deal with it again. Clearly, that was just wishful thinking. This injury is sticking with me until the end, it seems.

That afternoon, the hits started coming. Not literally, but close enough. As I ran past a shopping center, a woman sped out of the parking lot without yielding or *even* looking. I planted my feet and came to an abrupt stop and watched in disbelief as the car flew by *right* in front of me. It was a sobering reminder of why I need to stay focused until the very end of the run.

In case the lesson didn't sink in; soon after, another heedless driver pulled out of a shopping center without a glance. This time, I leaped out of the way just before the car plowed into me.

Just as I was getting my heart-rate down to a normal level, the same thing happened a third time and left me scrambling to get out of the way. At that point, I was furious and gave the car a "love tap" with the palm of my hand as it drove past. I was now desperate to be finished with the run, preferably by getting my miles in, not by getting run over.

As I continued on, my energy started to wane. Was it the heat and humidity? It wasn't as warm today as it had been, but it was still humid. It could also have been the busy roads and uninspiring surroundings. That does tend to lower my morale and suck the life out of me. Then again, so does nearly getting run over ... on three separate occasions.

Running on sidewalks all day long didn't help either. As I've mentioned before, it's both a positive and a negative. Well, today it seemed I received only the negative aspects of it. Sometime during my "triple-death scare," I developed pain in my left heel. The rest of my foot (actually, the rest of both of them) wasn't feeling great either. It's a good thing I have unlimited rest days coming up.

It wasn't until late afternoon that the city sprawl dwindled. By that time, I was out of gas and lumbering along in pain. Whatever enthusiasm I woke up with was long gone. And as much as I wanted to get the day over with, I didn't have the energy or the strength to speed up the process. I had to suffer through another couple of

349

grueling hours before my weary and ailing body managed to get me to the day's ending point, the Floridian Hotel. Clearly, it was a frustrating, dangerous, and painful "last before the last" day.

Running as far as I have, days like this were inevitable. If I hadn't experienced them, I probably wouldn't fully appreciate days like yesterday. I also wouldn't value tomorrow as much as I do. Despite everything I've been through, by this time tomorrow I'll be finished my 93-day, 14-state, 1,935-mile East Coast charity run. It's a mouthful, I know. Even though I haven't quite processed it all yet, the significance of this achievement isn't lost on me. I've had too many days like today not to realize it, and too many close calls (three today) not to recognize how very fortunate I am.

Day 93 (12/9/14): Homestead, FL to Key Largo, FL [24 miles]

At last, here it was. The final day of my East Coast charity run. All that remained before reaching Key Largo was one last run of 24 miles. I was super excited to get out there and finish up. I was also happy that my parents were here to cheer me on and see the finish. I only wish Ida and Jenna could be here as well. Unfortunately, Jenna has been suffering severe migraines as of late (one of the many complications of Sturge-Weber syndrome). So, Ida wanted to stay close to home and close to Dr. Anne Comi and the Kennedy Krieger Institute should any further problems arise. Despite my disappointment, they were with me in spirit as they have been throughout my journey.

Today was to be a busy day with a tight schedule. The Key Largo Chamber of Commerce had arranged for students from the Coral Shores High School track and cross-country teams to run with me the last few miles. They also planned a celebratory reception after I finished. Oh, and they lined up a police escort as well. It was all very nice, though I hoped the police officer driving the patrol car wasn't like Officer Steve from Maine. I'd prefer to end the run without another injury.

Al DeCesaris

As I readied for the day, congratulatory messages from friends, loved ones, and families affected by Sturge-Weber syndrome poured in. I can't stress enough how much these messages, and all the messages I received throughout the run, mean to me. When you're doing a charity event, a little encouragement goes a long way.

According to my schedule, I wasn't to arrive in Key Largo until 5pm, so I waited until late morning before setting out. Beyond what the Chamber of Commerce had planned, I wasn't sure what the day had in store for me. For certain, the heat and humidity wouldn't be a factor. It was cloudy and temps were in the low 70s.

From the start, I was full of energy and got through Homestead and Florida City, just to the south, in record time. I was so pumped up, I even found myself singing aloud as I ran. Thank goodness, there was no one around to hear me. Then again, I didn't care if anyone heard. This was my victory lap, and I meant to enjoy it.

An hour into my run, I came to the "18-Mile Stretch." It's the section of Route 1 that runs along the Southern Glades Wildlife and Environmental Area and connects the Florida mainland to the Florida Keys. Just beyond the Stretch's turquoise-painted barriers and chain-link fences were wetlands of sawgrass marshes, marl prairies, and tree islands. The Southern Glades are also home to a vast assortment of flora and wildlife including the Florida panther and the American crocodile. It's also home to snakes. Not far down the road, I came across a big one. Fortunately, it appeared about as interested in

Running The Coast For A Cure

me as I was in it. The plan for the day didn't include me getting rushed to the hospital with a snake bite.

As I flew down the Stretch, I soon realized that this was one of those special kinds of days where I was hitting on all cylinders. I felt like I could run forever. The back and heel pains I suffered through yesterday weren't bothering me at all. In truth, I don't think a broken leg would have bothered me today.

My zeal had me running much faster than I normally do. If I had kept up that pace, I would have reached Key Largo well before 5pm. Even though I wanted to continue running hard, I knew I had to take it down a notch (or several). So, I walk for a while to kill time.

When I resumed running, I passed a guy on a bicycle with panniers hanging from his bike rack. Where was he headed? Lubec, Maine? If you recall, not long after I started the run, I met a cyclist, who was about to finish his cross-country ride. Well, maybe here it was again; as one journey ends, another begins.

Farther down the road, just behind the fence, I saw a baby crocodile, or maybe it was a 'gator. Whichever it was (and regardless of the fact that it was just "fun-size"), its teeth looked like they could do some serious damage. And to think, I was worried about a snakebite.

About 16 miles in, the marshland along the roadway gave way to blue waters. Through this area, Route 1 rested on a narrow strip of land. It was evident I was closing in on the tropical archipelago known as the Florida Keys.

353

Al DeCesaris

Around 4:30pm, I reached the bridge that spans both Jewfish Creek and Lake Surprise and extends to my final destination, Key Largo. Despite the late start and the walking break, I was still ahead of schedule. So, I stepped to the side of the road and waited.

Although at the time I wished I had coordinated my arrival a little better, I'm now glad I had those few minutes before the finish to reflect on it all. It had been a long, arduous journey with extreme challenges and a number of serious injuries. Despite all the adversities, I managed to run (and, at times, limp) from Lubec, Maine all the way to Key Largo, Florida.

I realize I couldn't have done it alone. The support and encouragement of many people helped make this possible. And the blessings of the good Lord along with the inspiration of one beautiful little girl made it a reality.

After my roadside reflection, I continued on. When I got to the top of the bridge, I saw a police car ahead and five teenagers in running gear. I reached them a couple of minutes later and brief introductions were made. The students and I then ran the remainder of the way with the police car following behind with lights flashing.

Past the bridge, the road turned to the right and I caught sight of my parents and several students from Coral Shores High School in the median with a banner that read, "Congratulations Al on Running The Coast For A Cure." Behind them stood a big, colorful sign welcoming travelers to Key Largo.

Minutes later, the Coral Shores track and cross-country team runners and I reached the welcome sign.

354

Running The Coast For A Cure

And I reached my final destination, Key Largo. After congratulatory hugs and high-fives, we situated ourselves in front of the welcome sign for a photo. You didn't think I was going to run 1,935 miles and end this thing without a triumphant road sign pic, did you?

Al DeCesaris, his parents: Rose Mary and Albert DeCesaris and students from Coral Shores High School in Key Largo, Florida (photo courtesy of Julie Marshall).

We then ran to the Key Largo Chamber of Commerce Visitor Center just down the road. As the students and I entered the parking lot, members of the Chamber and a representative from the Mayor's Office cheered me on. My parents, the other students, and a few of the students' parents soon joined us. Everyone was super excited for me and couldn't have been more welcoming.

I was then presented with a Mayor's Proclamation commemorating the successful completion of my *Running The Coast For A Cure* – East Coast charity run.

We then headed inside the Visitor Center for the reception. While enjoying the company of new friends, I shared stories of my run. Also, I explained how I had taken on this journey in hopes of furthering the efforts to find a cure for Jenna and all those living with Sturge-Weber syndrome. I ran so they might have a better life. The funny thing is, I wouldn't have been able to run down the entire East Coast, or bike across America for that matter, without Jenna inspiring me. She gave me purpose as well as the strength and will to fight on her behalf. When you think about it, we both played a significant role in this.

Together, we are making great strides toward a cure.

Al DeCesaris and Jenna Heck
(image courtesy of Bill Whitcher).

AUTHOR'S NOTE

Thank you for purchasing and reading *Running The Coast For A Cure.* Through your generous support, we're creating more awareness about Sturge-Weber syndrome every day and raising critical funds for medical research.

To further support the cause, please share *Running The Coast For A Cure* on social media and recommend it to your family and friends. Also, let them know that ALL profits from the sale of this book fund Sturge-Weber syndrome research.

Another great way to help is to post a book review online (www.amazon.com and/or www.goodreads.com). Amazon book reviews are especially important. They're not only relied on by people when making purchasing decisions, but Amazon uses the number of reviews and star rating to determine which books to recommend to their customers. Reviews help spread the word and help raise greater awareness about Sturge-Weber syndrome.

Together we are giving hope to those suffering with Sturge-Weber syndrome and inspiring others to join the fight against this devastating neurological disorder!

With sincere thanks,

Al DeCesaris

ABOUT THE AUTHOR

Al DeCesaris in Hillsboro Beach, Florida (photo courtesy of Shawn Vernon).

Since 2006, Al DeCesaris has volunteered his time and dedicated his efforts to raising awareness and funds for the research and treatment of Sturge-Weber syndrome, a rare neurological disorder that afflicts his niece Jenna.

In 2013, he bicycled solo 3,088 miles from Santa Monica, California to Ocean City, Maryland in honor of Jenna and subsequently published a book about his ride, *Crossing America For A Cure: A Bicycle Journey Of Inspiration And Hope*. In 2014, he took on another incredibly challenging endeavor, this time on foot. Running solo close to a marathon a day for three consecutive months, he covered 1,935 miles as he made his way from Lubec, Maine to Key Largo, Florida.

Through his athletic endeavors, charity events, and books, Al has created considerable awareness about the disorder and helped raise significant funds for medical research. His efforts have brought hope to his niece and those suffering with Sturge-Weber syndrome and have inspired others to help those in need.

Al DeCesaris

To further the efforts to find a cure, Al DeCesaris is dedicating all profits from the sale of his "For A Cure" books to Sturge-Weber syndrome research.

To learn more, please visit www.AlDeCesaris.com

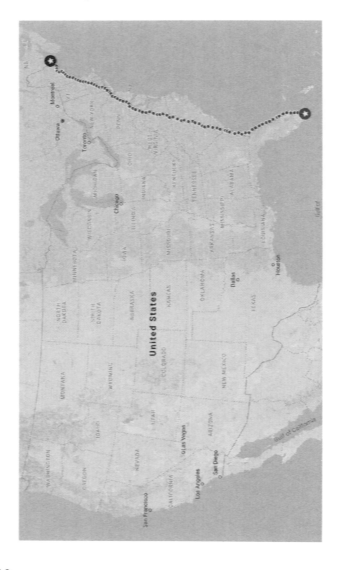

Made in the USA
Columbia, SC
18 January 2019